To Li'l
Princess

Noel
NOEL

# TRACTION

## THE LIFE AND LEGACY OF NOEL CROXON

Sheilagh Croxon
with
Claire Carver-Dias

# TRACTION

## THE LIFE AND LEGACY OF NOEL CROXON

*This book is dedicated to Sarah, Grace, Anna, Addy,*
*Lucas, Marley, Natalie and Nicolas.*

## The Clock of Life

*The clock of life is wound but once,*
*And no man has the power*
*To tell just when the hands will stop*
*At late or early hour.*

*To lose one's wealth is sad indeed,*
*To lose one's health is more,*
*To lose one's soul is such a loss*
*That no man can restore.*

*The present only is our own,*
*So live, love, toil with a will --*
*Place no faith in 'Tomorrow' --*

*For the clock may then be still.*

Robert H. Smith

# The Ignition

· · · · ·

Clock of Life was recited by my father, Noel Croxon, at my wedding twenty-five years ago. It has always been one of my dad's favourite poems and its message is a simple but powerful one: to live a meaningful life. This book is inspired by that sentiment as much as by the incredible tale of Noel Croxon's life and legacy. So many other themes rose to the surface as I began to listen more closely to my dad's stories, and plan this project. While the clock was the initial inspiration, the enduring image that tied this project together – perhaps because of Noel's impenetrable perseverance or perhaps because of his undeniable success in the car industry — are vehicle metaphors. My dad was and continues to be driven. His life achievements and philosophy have had traction in my own life. It became my heartfelt desire to turn the key in the ignition and explore the pathways of Noel's life.

Fortunately, as I write this, my dad is in excellent health, both physically and mentally, for which I am truly grateful. I am thankful for the impact he has had on my life, his unconditional support, sound advice, and dedication to hard work. I'm awestruck by his remarkable personal story of struggle and triumph. I am also thankful for the support of Claire Carver-Dias throughout this project – without her gift of writing, this book may not have become a reality.

Noel's life started out on a bumpy road. Born into poverty and a fractured family, he had to battle to gain traction early on. But he pressed down his heel and trekked onward. His narrative tells of the forward pull of ambition, the driving power of hard work, and an unwillingness to put on the brakes. For Noel, these qualities aren't forced; they're simply a natural part of who he is.

The book includes contemporary vignettes that occurred during the process of writing, as well as stories and memories from individuals closest to Noel. What I didn't expect to uncover when we set out on this creative journey was just how much Noel's character traits, beliefs, and habits have been passed down to Bruce, Michael, and me, his three children. It's my hope that through sharing his remarkable story, my dad's lessons will find traction in and enrich the lives of others as well.

For Noel: May you experience immense pleasure as you read and reread your life's story, basking in your many accomplishments and the impact you have had on so many. May you be delighted by the questions of your grandchildren as they inquire with curiosity about aspects of your life story.

Finally, may you grow old with satisfaction in your heart, knowing that you've taught all of us the art of driving – that our journeys will be a lot smoother because of you.

Plant trees for your great-grandchildren -
for future generations.

Create the legacy of a better world.

Leave this world a better place than you found it.

Jonathan Lockwood Huie

# PART ONE

· · · · ·

## Learning to Drive

# Chapter One

# Early Roads

· · · · ·

His father's second-hand Rover rumbled along an old dirt road between an open field and a hawthorne hedge on its daily journey towards the outskirts of London. Four-year-old Noel Croxon knelt on the back seat to peek out the side window of the car, hoping to see the burgeoning suburbs beyond the hedge. It seemed like new rows of houses grew daily in those vast green farm fields, the city quickly over-spilling its boundaries. Today the hedge had grown too high, so Noel turned his focus to the road ahead, visible between his silent parents, Cranmer and Josephine, known as Cran and Jo, in the front seat. He counted the cars – bright shades of green, red, and blue, barrelling towards them on the narrow road. With each one, his father would slow, pull over a little, wait for them to pass, then continue through the clouds of grey-brown dust.

As the car neared the private housing estate where they would sell their wares, it rattled over the bumpy divide where the country roadway abruptly switched to a smoother, newer surface. Instinctively, Noel glanced through the back window to check whether the large wooden crate his father had affixed to the car was still in place. And there it was, firmly intact, thanks to his father's skilled carpentry, with its varied cargo of home-grown and store-bought vegetables, eggs, and poultry, safely protected beneath a blanket. Noel turned to fix his eyes on the road ahead, absorbing the thrill of forward movement.

They pulled to a stop at the bottom of a hilly street lined with spindly trees and pebbledash-clad semi-detached homes, and his parents quickly hopped out. Jo checked her reflection in the window, primped her white-blond hair, and straightened her brown frock before proceeding to the wooden crate. Cran was already there, carefully folding back the blanket cover, pulling out a large turnip and carrot bunch. Jo scurried up the pavement to a house on the opposite side of the street. Noel stayed inside the now steaming car and watched his parents work.

Cran made his way past a wooden gate to a glistening navy blue front door. He had a laboured sort of gait, favouring his left foot as he walked. Recently, Noel and his older brother, known as Cran Jr., had noticed the way their father grunted and hopped a little as he moved, but said nothing about it, because their father said nothing. Cran Sr. simply limped from whatever task needed to be done to the next task without any evidence of self-pity. Later the boys, and their older sister, Yvonne, would learn that their father's lop-sided walk was due to Syringomyelia, a chronic and painful progressive disease affecting the spinal cord. Despite battling pain and increasing weakness, he never complained, and continued to approach every business endeavour with unwavering dedication and elbow grease.

Noel's father knocked on the door of the home and brushed away the dirt on the carrots as he waited. From his backseat perch, Noel smiled when a woman appeared in the doorway and Cran began to speak, holding up the waxy purple turnip, the woman tilting her head in interest. Noel knew his father hoped to sell a lot of produce today; that's why his mother had come along to help. When the woman at the door disappeared into the house for a moment, surely to collect her purse, Cran turned to glance at Noel, giving a small, serious nod.

Hours later, the crate was finally empty. Cran collapsed into the front seat, and began hastily to count coins, while Noel leaned over the back rest, doing his best to add up the total in his head.

There was a moment of quiet, a quick sigh, then Cran spoke: "It's just not enough to pay the rent." Those were words Noel's father must have uttered to Jo several times before, when one or another of his business ventures failed to produce enough money to sustain their family of five. But each time, Cran would regroup and move on.

There was no time to wallow. Instead, Jo tucked away the money, and Cran pulled the car into gear. They unwound their way out of the glossy newness of the estate, and rode back over the bump in the narrowing roadway into the kicked-up dust of fancier automobiles. They sped past the farmer's field where Cran had worked as a tractor driver at the time of Noel's birth, on Christmas Day of 1927, and finally arrived home at their tiny cottage, Purleigh Mill.

Noel's earliest memories centred on this little cottage, its dark corners unreached by the light of oil lamps and candles. There was no running water and only an outside toilet to which Noel stumbled in the deep dark of the countryside night.

The little chicken farm adjacent to the property was filled with noisy clucking and a putrid stench. Noel's father had used money given to him by Jo's brother to buy equipment and supplies to help maintain the operation, but they still couldn't make ends meet. Often Noel had rushed out when he heard the panicked newborn-like cries of a chicken picked up for slaughter; he wanted to see if he could help pluck it afterwards. Sometimes he was allowed, but inevitably, halfway through his meticulous plucking, an adult had taken over, impatient and eager to prepare the fowl for the market. Soon they would be moving away from all this. At the time, Noel wasn't aware that this situation was about to change – but moving would become a way of life for the Croxon family.

Eating the poultry they raised was a luxury the family could not afford. It was always rabbit for them. Most evenings Noel and his brother would accompany their father on rabbiting outings. Scratching and sniffing, their dog would seek out a warren. Then the boys would carefully lay down netting over its various exits, place a ferret on a lead down one of the holes, and wait to capture the rabbit as it was chased out of its lair into a catch-net. After Noel's father broke the animal's neck, they'd swiftly move on to the next burrow. Later on, Cran skinned the game and passed it along to Jo to be prepared. Stewing was her go-to method. Noel never dreamed of complaining about the meals she laid before them at suppertime. Hungry, he gobbled up the chewy, lean meat with scarcely a word uttered, but would later come to avoid the animal entirely.

Noel loved to kneel at his father's side as he worked in his garden. Its rows were orderly and bright, unlike the crammed, shadowy space of the cottage. When Cran first crouched in the earth he winced, but then he would begin to dig and plant and move along and weed and cultivate luscious, colourful things.

One day, as Noel followed his father's systematic movement through the garden, he spotted his brother racing a bicycle along the cottage road and crunching to a dramatic stop. Noel jumped up and joined him, studying the moves, then taking his first turn. He pushed with his feet, attempting to find balance, lifted one shoe off the ground, then the other, wobbling along, with his brother running at his side, cheering. He thought he had the hang of it, moving steadily along. Suddenly the wheel skidded out from underneath him and Noel tumbled to the stony, muddy road. He sat for a moment, smeared with dirt and scraped badly, close to tears, and thought about calling out to his father. Only a short distance away Cran wiped his brow, and limped to begin weeding the next garden row. Noel bit his lip, stood, swung his bloodied leg over the bike, and tried again.

## Sheilagh's Kitchen. May 12, 2016

*On this day in my kitchen, Noel fidgets in his chair as we interrogate him about these first memories. He travelled here alone, battling Toronto's horrendous rush-hour traffic, from his new condo on the other side of the city, but does not complain about the commute. Nor does he mention his arthritis as he shifts in his seat in front of us. More than eight decades later it seems that the gritty determination of that young boy on the bike isn't far away. Noel still craves movement. He does not like to be in one spot for too long, plucks at the corners of the papers in front of him, checks the clock, and charges through our questions without pause. Even the emotional scrapes of certain life events are not dwelled upon too heavily. While the pain of some events is acknowledged, Noel is ever 'swinging his leg back over the bike' and moving along.*

The Croxons did not remain at Purleigh Mill for long. In an effort to save on rent, they packed up their few belongings and moved to another farm nearby.

Noel felt the laneway to the new cottage would never end. On one side there was an orchard, the apples ripe for the picking, and at its end was their cottage, another dilapidated place with no running water nor electricity. Shortly after their arrival, Noel and his brother snuck off to collect some fruit. They stood below one tree, straining to pluck any of the shiny specimens off the branches, but they were beyond their reach. Unwilling to give up, the brothers went searching for something to use to knock down the apples. Among their father's things, they found a tool with spikes on its end, used mainly for breaking up clumps of soil when gardening. Noel clutched the instrument and ran ahead, as fast as he could, back to the tree, barely stopping before he began swinging at the lowest fruit. He jumped and whipped the tool forcefully, wildly, towards a branch and felt it make contact. No apple fell. But Cran Jr. did. He slumped to his knees holding his forehead, a thin stream of blood trickling down between his fingers and down his forearm.

They made their way back to their new cottage, Cran Jr. holding his hand against his head, and Noel worried about the trouble he might be in. As they skulked closer, it dawned on Cran Jr., one year older than Noel, that he was equally implicated in the act, so he stood a little taller and stopped whimpering. He wasn't as hurt as they'd originally thought. And now they both braced for discipline. When they entered the cottage, chins dipped, Jo moved quickly to inspect the bloodied forehead. Cran Sr. listened to the boys' story and looked closely at the apologetic faces. No punishment was levied, simply a stern and justified lecture about the danger of playing with tools.

Their time at the long-lane orchard cottage, called The Crib, was short-lived. Within the year, Noel's father found a job in Abbess Roding, working part-time as a farm hand, tending to cattle and driving a tractor. On the side, he continued to sell produce in the London suburbs. The family settled into a small home on the property, and five-year old Noel prepared to join his siblings at the local school.

Each morning the Croxon children made the three-kilometre trek to their school of forty students. Even as a five-year-old, Noel worked to stay on pace with his siblings, pedalling or speed-walking the bumpy route to their hilltop schoolhouse where he would take his place beside clever Brenda Neville. She was quick to raise her hand and provide the responses that made the teacher nod with approval. Noel noticed her intelligence, and it lit a spark of competitiveness in him. He did whatever he could to keep up with her.

Noel's strong start at school hinted at a budding intellect and an uncanny skill for memorization that he would nurture throughout his life, reciting poetry and charming (or shocking) limericks at every occasion.

## Sheilagh's Kitchen. May 20, 2016

*Back in my kitchen, Noel is determined to recite Marriott Edgar's "The Lion and Albert" in its entirety. Halfway through the seventh stanza, he pauses, scratches his cheek. I try to intervene and begin to say, "It's okay Dad …" but he holds up his hand and cuts me off, continuing his recitation. This seems to be a competition for him – against time and the fickleness of memory. Determined, he ploughs through to the final perfectly-recited word, and finally sits back and smiles.*

*A week or so later, back in my kitchen, Noel recites the alphabet backwards rapidly for us and asks us if we can do it. Neither Claire nor I can. He taught himself this trick at the age of ten, in order to keep up with his older sister, Yvonne, who had learned it from friends. It remains filed in his brain, precise and impressive.*

At Christmastime of his kindergarten year, Noel was selected to recite an adaptation of a Beatrix Potter poem during the school's holiday performance at the church hall. The words of the short verse were quickly engraved in his head. On the evening of the performance, not yet six years old, Noel stood mid-stage, one hundred-plus eyes glued on him, cleared his throat and spoke out in a clear voice:

*I had a little garden, all my very own.*
*I had to plant everything, and did it all alone.*
*I used to plant potatoes, and did it in a row.*
*Although I dug them up each day, they never seem to grow.*

The audience applauded heartily.

Although Noel began to flourish at school, life did not get any easier for the family. They moved again for Noel's father to take on another farm-hand role at Hunter's Hall Farm in Epping Green. Cran's physical and financial health continued to deteriorate. He had been forced to give up his door-to-door produce sales business and automobile for good now. Despite his restricted ability, Cran carefully planted and tended to a new garden on the property. From seed, he grew many vegetables including potatoes, carrots, Brussels sprouts, cabbage, radish, lettuce, tomatoes, and cucumbers. The silhouette of his crooked body stood slightly taller, prouder, amidst the flourishing plants.

The farm owners required two labourers; at least one of them needed to be physically capable. To make up for Cran's ailing body, they hired a tall, athletic, and handsome young man named Wally. He came to live with the family in their small semi-detached home on the farm property. It was a humble place: the family had to hand-pump their water from a well, and all cooking was done from either a primus stove or the main fireplace in the living room. The toilet was twenty yards from the home outside, and often, when Noel rushed out the back door to use it, he would spot Wally, his muscled arms crossed against his broad chest, laughing and chatting with Jo, who puffed daintily on a cigarette.

Around this time, Noel's father began to make regular trips into London where he had found a way to make a few extra pounds serving as a guinea pig for the doctors at Guy's Hospital. Clipboards in hand, medical students studied the progress of his incurable disease, poking and prodding his body, taking measurements, making observations in the third person as though Cran was not there. Noel would watch his father leave for these appointments, moving slowly down the lane on his five-kilometre journey to the bus stop from where he would catch a ride to London. He walked alone, face fixed on the horizon, forever limping forward.

Noel admired the determination in his father's slow steps. He was proud of Cran's ability to keep pushing forward, to make ends meet. To find streaks of hope in the mud.

Chapter Two

# Traction

· · · · ·

**Sheilagh's Kitchen. October 5, 2017**

*When we gather next in my kitchen, we begin our conversation by speaking about Noel's parents' relationship. There is no change in his steady serious voice as we venture into his recollections of later childhood, but there is a stark shift away from the disparate carefree tableaux of his earliest memories. The curtain on simple innocence is lowered, and raised on a more complicated narrative, punctuated by family strife, an approaching war, and a gradual exploration of his own potential.*

Late one night Noel awoke to the sound of a loud exchange downstairs, followed by the clatter of a chair hitting the ground. As he crept out of bed, his father's normally calm voice rose aggressively above the cacophony: "How dare you?"

Noel swung around the corner and practically slid down the stairs into the dimly lit but noisy scene. Cran Jr. and Yvonne stood wide-eyed, their backs pressed against the wall on one side of the living room, watching their father swing violently at Wally, who ducked out of the way, then lunged forward and delivered a hard blow to Cran's midriff. Jo waved her long arms frantically in the air and begged the men to stop. Throughout the scuffle, their angry words continued. From what Noel could piece together that night, and through overhearing whispers in the days that followed, his father had set out for Guy's Hospital that afternoon, claiming he would be staying in town overnight to be ready for an early morning appointment. But he had returned unexpectedly, perhaps intentionally, and had found Jo and Wally in each other's arms.

That night, Noel's father had held his fists high, eyes afire, as the children looked on. Even fuelled by rage, Cran, with his slight frame and weakened state, would never stand a chance against this large and athletic opponent. They all knew it.

Suddenly, Jo raised her voice: "The children. The children." It was a plea to the men to give up their battle. And it worked. They lowered their clenched fists and stepped apart.

Noel's father turned to his three kids, chin down, eyes averted. "Go to bed, children," he said under his breath. From that point on there were no more sounds, except the soft padding of little feet quickly climbing the staircase and slipping under covers.

The next day Wally and all his belongings had disappeared from the house and property. Without Wally's strength behind him, Cran struggled to complete his farm work. It was not long before Noel's father was fired from his farm hand role, and the family faced another move.

In the weeks that followed, the house was filled with the fierce whispers of Noel's parents, as they planned their separation. Noel did not really understand what was happening, he simply felt that things had shifted. There was the shadow of that night lingering in the rift between his parents.

Seven-year-old Noel, his siblings, and Jo prepared to move again, this time without Cran Sr. Packing was quite easy since they owned so little; Noel tucked his pajamas and single change of clothes into a sack, put on his solitary pair of shoes, and collected his prized possession, his bicycle. His brother joined him outside and they set out on bikes in the general direction of Ongar, where they would be living in a small flat with their mother. The two boys, just seven and eight years old, pedalled ferociously down the lanes, doing their best to continue in the direction of their new village. At each crossroad, they checked for road signs, sometimes stopping to pull back greenery and unveil hidden posts. They kept going and going. Noel's legs were tiring quickly, but he did not complain. Hours later, they somehow, miraculously, arrived at the right place.

Penniless and increasingly weak, Noel's father managed to mastermind a move of his own. No longer in a position to rent the Epping Green house and eager to find a more permanent dwelling, he turned to the British Legion. During the First World War, he had been a prisoner of war, captured from the trenches in France and taken to Germany as a prisoner where he worked unloading ships in the Kiel Canal until the war ended. Because of his service and imprisonment, he was eligible to receive financial assistance. They paid him a sum of one-hundred pounds, a portion of which he used to purchase an old horse-drawn bus. Legion members found a place for Cran to park the vehicle, in the field at the top of a laneway at Little Weald Hall, near North Weald. He then used his carpentry skills to fix up and furnish the four-hundred square feet of space inside, transforming it into a liveable area.

Upon every visit to his father's home, Noel noticed little changes. Cran had acquired some couches and beds and had nurtured yet another thriving vegetable garden. He had also purchased another shack, about three-hundred square feet, to use for cooking and eating. Noel would hurry to help when his father struggled back to the caravan carrying heavy pails of water from the nearest source of running water.

Life in Ongar went on as well. Noel, Cran Jr., and Yvonne entered new schools while Jo earned some money house cleaning. She also continued to see Wally. One evening, she instructed Noel to follow her on a bike journey. They moved quickly down miles of roadway, a car or two passing by and engulfing them in dust, and finally arrived at their destination. They balanced their bikes against the wall of a building. Wally stood, street-side, waiting for them. He tousled Noel's hair as Jo pointed to a bench nearby. "Wait there and do not move until we return," she instructed Noel, sternly.

Noel obeyed. He kicked his legs back and forth, and watched their backs as they crossed the road, and disappeared hand-in-hand into a nearby field. A while later, Jo emerged, they mounted their bicycles and returned to Ongar.

This happened regularly. Often their long bike rides led them to new villages – wherever Wally was working that evening. The adults would traipse into the green fields and Noel would sit and wait.

One morning, Jo pressed four pennies into Noel's palm and sent him out to get her usual pack of ten cigarettes. The bell on the store door jingled as Noel entered. Drooling, he surveyed the shelves laden with jars of colourful candies. One day he hoped he would have enough change to buy a treat of his own. He purchased his mother's cigarettes and left. As he passed by the next store's doorway, a lady's voice called out from inside,

"Young man, come in here!" she said. Noel looked around to see if she might be addressing someone else, but found that no one else was around. Slowly, he pushed open the door and walked towards the woman. She was alone, an apron tied around her waist.

"I need you to buy these things for me," she said, holding out a piece of paper and some coins. "Here's the money to buy the items from other shops. Once you're done, come back with the goods."

Noel hesitated, but then grasped the list and money, and set to work moving from store to store to collect the items. When he returned, the woman paid him a few pennies for his efforts. He squeezed the money tight in his fist. He liked the sensation of doing a chore and getting paid for it.

The very next day, Noel walked extra slowly, and hopefully, past the woman's store, waiting to see what would happen. She called out to him again. This time he rushed in.

"Come by every day to see if I have errands for you to run," she said.

At seven years old, Noel had his first job.

# Chapter Three

# The Hands of Time

· · · · ·

Regularly, Noel and his brother would cycle the eight kilometres over rough roads to their father's caravan. When they were there, they played in the streams and fields, but occasionally they would accompany Cran on visits to relatives. One of Noel's favourite places to visit was the home of an aunt and uncle, whose kindness became etched in memory, but whose names and faces were eventually lost in the grey dust of passing time. They were gentle people, always quick to offer tea and biscuits to the ever-ravenous young boys. What captivated Noel during those visits was the row of pocket watches hung carefully on the parlour wall. One was a shining gold open-face model, another a tarnished silver hunter-case. Yet another was adorned with elaborate carved detail. Noel longed to hold one of them in his hands, to feel the light pulse of its relentless tick-tick-tick, to monitor the hands in constant circular movement.

Feeling a surge of boldness on one of their visits, Noel said, "I would very much like to have a pocket watch." His uncle and aunt had looked at one another in amusement.

Cran Sr. quickly stepped in, "Now Noel, mind your manners."

The adults had then turned away from the two boys, continued sipping their tea and resumed their heated discussion about the distressing events beginning to unfold in Germany. Noel returned his gaze to the watch wall.

Upon their next visit to these relatives, Noel gravitated once again to the display. He loved everything about the time pieces: the gleam of the metal, the sound of their movement, the mystery beneath the watch face, their practicality. While Noel stood admiring the watches, his uncle walked up beside him.

Noel saw this as his chance. If he didn't ask for what he wanted, he might never get it. "May I have one?" he said. "Please."

The uncle chuckled, patted Noel's head, and reached out to pluck a silver watch off the wall. Noel could hardly believe this was actually happening. The uncle unfurled Noel's hand, placed the beautiful piece in his palm and said, "It's yours now, young man." Noel felt the delightful ticking against his skin.

## Father's Day. June 18, 2017

*This Father's Day we arranged to have dinner with my dad at one of his favourite restaurants near his home. He insisted that my brother Bruce and my husband Jean accompany Lucas and Nicolas, Noel's two grandsons, for a short visit to his house before the dinner.*

*When they arrive, they are greeted by a display of Noel's twenty-plus watches, all laid out neatly on the table. Noel explains that he wants his grandsons to have these watches, and that some are very old and valuable. Lucas and Nicolas' eyes light up as they listen to their grandfather's stories about how he acquired some of the most valuable ones. A particular specimen was gifted to Noel by his long-time switchboard operator when she retired as a 'thank you' to him for being such a great employer. Another was given to him by the contractors who built the auto complex at Yonge and Steeles, where he worked for years. Many were purchased at antique shops and markets during Noel's numerous trips back to England.*

It was around that time that Jo stopped her evening visits to the fields where Wally worked. She had even begun to accompany the children on their bike rides to the caravan to visit their father. It was not long before Cran and Jo announced that they would be getting back together, and that the family would be under the same roof again. The five Croxons crammed into Cran's tiny caravan and wooden shack. To create more space, they erected two tents outside; Noel and his brother slept in one, Yvonne in the other.

Not long after, Jo and Cran welcomed another baby into the family, a little boy named Leo. The caravan became more chaotic with the squawks of an infant, and Noel found great pleasure in being outside and engaging in the hard work of digging up potatoes, picking beans, and driving the horses and carts on the farm property where they lived.

Noel attended North Weald Junior School and thrived in the classroom. His teacher, Mr. Brinn, praised him for his prowess in arithmetic and memorization. When Mr. Brinn dismissed the students for breaks or at the day's end, Noel would run outside and play cricket boisterously, using a borrowed bat, with his buddies on the uneven, rocky meadow near the school. They bowled and shouted, racing about with wide grins on their faces, but the fun and friendship remained in the yard. Noel never invited his chums home with him. In addition to the caravan being too out of the way, he didn't want his schoolmates to see their tiny, noisy home. The short row of tattered shoes inside the door. Their poverty.

Buoyed by the successful results of boldly asking his uncle for the pocket watch, Noel approached Mr. Brinn in the schoolyard one day and asked if he would purchase him a cricket bat. The teacher smiled and did not respond, but came to school a few days later with a bat. In exchange, Noel dug into his pocket and produced two shillings.

"Thank you, young man," said Mr. Brinn as he gracefully accepted the coins, not divulging any hint that it was an uneven exchange. Eager to try out this new equipment, Noel ran out to the field to play with his friends.

A few weeks later the generous Mr. Brinn offered to take Noel and two of his friends to Chelmsford to watch a cricket match between the British West Indies and Essex, featuring the great Leary Constantine and George Headley. The three students piled into the teacher's Austin, and, despite a flat tire repair on the way, made it to the pitch in time to enjoy a marvellous game.

Noel's time at the junior school came to a close and he joined his older siblings at the senior school, a ten-kilometre bike ride from home. Although Mr. Brinn was no longer a part of Noel's daily life, his acts of generosity were stamped upon Noel's memory, just as were the benevolent uncle's. Noel began to see how he could pull himself out of the chaos growing around him. How in the midst of the early murmurings of war, the tension between his parents, and the family's constant struggle against poverty, he could work hard and boldly ask for help. He could jump on his bike and pedal away from the mud-locked caravan, in pursuit of the opportunities on the horizon.

If you're going through hell,
keep going.

Winston Churchill

# Chapter Four

# Let It Roll

· · · · ·

The family huddled around the radio in the caravan straining to hear the BBC baritone beyond the static. Noel's father reached forward, adjusting the knob.

Losing interest as his father struggled with the set, Noel looked about the room. By the door sat their shoes, recently patched by Cran. Above the neatly placed pairs hung several cardboard boxes on strings. Before school broke for the summer, Noel had to drape the box around his neck to take to class each morning. Squeezed inside were standard issue gas masks everyone had been taught to strap on quickly in the event of an air raid.

Noel's stomach growled. He craved bread, but there was none to spare as the rationing had already begun. His second-hand shirt, bought at the Epping Market to replace his old stained and ripped top, was itchy around the collar. He tugged at it.

Suddenly a tremulous voice emerged from the static. It was the new Prime Minister, Winston Churchill. Noel forgot about the gasmasks, the emergency drills he and his classmates had undergone daily throughout the year, and the cramped caravan in the summer humidity, and focused on the inspirational words channelling through the radio waves: "For my own part, looking out upon the future, I do not view the process with any misgivings. I could not stop it if I wished; no one can stop it. Like the Mississippi, it just keeps rolling along. Let it roll. Let it roll on full flood, inexorable, irresistible, benignant, to broader lands and better days."

There was something about this seemingly fearless leader that lifted Noel's spirits. Churchill spoke of the calamities already befallen the Allied Forces, but then called for courage, incited hope.

That night, as twelve-year-old Noel walked to his tent, he saw flashes and an orange glow on the horizon where the Germans were bombing London. The echo of Churchill's forceful words somehow cut through the terror.

North Weald had an aerodrome that housed both Spitfires and Hurricanes, the main fighter planes used by Great Britain in the war. Each summer morning, Noel cycled the perimeter of the airfield to get to work on the farm. He helped out in the cow shed, mainly collecting containers of fresh milk and biking them over to where they could be placed in coolers. One morning, Noel cycled across the property, with a can of milk balanced on his bike, when an aircraft dove out of the thick clouds, and then re-entered them. The milk teetered and splashed as Noel stopped to gaze upward. The plane appeared and disappeared again and again, and then was gone. Noel scratched his head and continued on. Later in the cowshed, one of the farm hands explained with a trembling voice that it had been a German aircraft taking photos of the aerodrome.

Noel returned home, glancing periodically at the clouds that hid England's enemy, and summoned up out of his memory one of Churchill's recent addresses:

"We shall defend our Island, whatever the cost may be, we shall fight on the beaches, we shall fight on the landing grounds, we shall fight in the fields and in the streets, we shall fight in the hills; we shall never surrender ..."

Noel's parents refused to surrender to the terror of the times as well. Cran and Jo had turned the shack next to the caravan into a café, which they kept open all hours, even though few customers entered during daylight. Cran had somehow managed to clamber up onto the roof and paint the word Café in large white letters. In the evenings, the airmen from the airfield would cram inside. The space would be filled with chatter and laughter, the light hammer of darts hitting the board, and the smell of cigarettes, fried eggs, bacon, and ham. Noel loved the buzz of the friendly crowd. On the occasions when he wasn't helping his parents, who had to prepare the food without the benefit of electricity, he delighted in sitting with the men and listening to their tales of travel and flight.

For Noel, the only shadows over this happy time were the moments when he would overhear his mother's giggle from around a corner and catch a glimpse of her hand lingering too long on the sleeve of an airman's coat. There was a driver who transported fuel oils, who stopped at the café one day. She rushed to serve him, her chin dropped and head tilted while they spoke. He returned several times after that, and Noel's mother insisted she could keep him company as he made his rounds to the neighbouring towns. She would slide her lean body into the cab of his truck, pulling her slim ankle languidly inside before the door clanked closed and the vehicle growled forward. Noel forced himself to turn away and continue whatever task he had begun.

Each afternoon the men at the farm where Noel worked sent him to purchase candy bars from a catering truck that drove around the airfield. One hot August afternoon, the truck didn't show up. Noel dismounted his bike and sat at the side of the runway, picking at blades of grass. The birds were suddenly silenced by the roar of a German bomber descending from the clouds, and Noel's ears were filled with a high-pitched whistling sound. He sprinted and dove into a nearby ditch as bombs exploded all across the property. He pressed his hands over his ears and watched as the air filled with smoke and debris. His heart racing and jaw sore from instinctive clamping, he waited until the bombs stopped and the sky seemed clear. Then he sprang up and ran and ran and ran, breathless, until strong arms wrapped around his waist and pulled him down flat to the ground.

"Stay down," said a man. Noel looked around. He was now

lying below a mobile antiaircraft gun that could not be fired because Allied fighters were in the air. He was surrounded by Army personnel. He remained there with them, silent and shaking until the area was deemed clear and they let him go.

In a mental fog, Noel somehow located his bike and wandered home. He didn't remember what path he took or whether he saw anyone along the way. He simply found himself home and, faced with the concerned looks of his parents, ate a bowl of rabbit stew.

For several days, Noel avoided the airstrip. He went to work, but did not dare to fetch candy bars for the workers. Eventually, a number of farmers convinced him it would be safe to go together. As the group reached the edge of the runway, almost exactly the spot where Noel had plucked at grass a few days earlier, the sound began. The roar and whistling and blasts all over again. It was a little more distant this time, but the sounds ripped through Noel. He lay down on the ground until the trembling stopped, then slowly made his way home, entered the house, and did not return to the airfield.

When school began just days later, Noel did not go. For two months, he found excuses to stay in a tight perimeter around the caravan, passing the time kicking stones into puddles, and observing his father in the garden. He found himself glancing up at the clouds every so often, immobilized by fear, imagining he heard a whistle. One morning Noel's mother took him by the hand and led him back to school, where he overheard her telling the headmaster that he'd been out of town visiting relatives over the previous weeks.

Once he took his place in the classroom, he fell easily back into the rhythm of learning. Memorizing poems and arithmetic occupied Noel's mind, and shook away some of the terror of the summer's end. He leaned into the comfort of repetition. With each muttering of a phrase, he grew stronger and less afraid.

Over the course of that year, the daytime bombing stopped, but then picked up at night time. Noel and his brother would stare at the roof of their tent each evening as the German bombers rumbled overhead, one after the other.

One day, Noel heard from one of the local farmhands that a damaged bomber had dropped a load of incendiary bombs into a field nearby the Croxon caravan. Immediately a clash of curiosity and terror built inside Noel. The next morning, he studied the clear sky, swallowed deeply and headed out to survey the bomb site. He walked slowly, reminding himself of the opportunity that might await him – parts of the debris might be valuable – and pushed the fear further down into his belly. Just off the path, the right place was evident due to the pock-marked earth and scorched grasses. Tentatively he circled each hole, peering down to see what lay in the mess of dirt and darkness. Heart pounding, Noel reached down into the pits to dig around. Buried deep in the soil were the inflammable remains of the bombs, steel tails, and fins. Touching the now-cool metal calmed Noel. It took him a couple of hours to wrestle all the remaining parts out of the depths. He then loaded the loot into a sack and carried it back to the airfield, humming along the way. At the end of the day he sold twenty fins to an airman for one shilling each.

Noel found other ways to make money. He took a job delivering milk in the village. For seven shillings a week, he would wake up at 5:30 a.m., ride his bicycle into the village, load two crates of bottled milk onto another bicycle, which had been adapted for that purpose. Noel would then travel around the area dropping off standing orders for daily milk. On Saturday and Sunday, he travelled with the milkman in his van to collect the money people owed him, then he would wash all the bottles and have them ready for the next day. Considerate of others, even in the cold weather, Noel slept in the tent, so his early wakeup would not disturb his family.

• • • •

**Michael Croxon.**
**Lessons from the Paper Route.**

*One of the early memories of my dad is his involvement in our paper routes as kids. Bruce, being the oldest, was the first to secure a route delivering "The Globe and Mail" in our neighbourhood, and Sheilagh and I followed suit once we were old enough to be out every morning in the dark. We ensured the residents of Guildwood Village had their paper on the doorstep when they woke up. My dad took a keen interest in our respective success in this, our first entrepreneurial venture. While the responsibility for getting ourselves out of bed, outside, and completing the route each morning was entirely our own, we always knew that our dad had our backs if something went wrong in the morning routine. And inevitably, stuff went wrong! Whether it was a particularly heavy snow storm, a mishap on the route, or simply sleeping through our alarms, if we ended up at our parents' bedroom door prior to departure, my dad's feet would be on the floor almost before we would knock to wake him and ask for help. And, while it did not necessarily happen often, he was always there to ensure we fulfilled our commitments to the Globe readers on Regency Square and surrounding streets.*

*The month of July always posed a challenge as each of us were privileged enough to attend overnight camp for that month. While other paper carriers would arrange for a friend to take over their routes for the month, we had our dad who willingly took over and ensured the papers were delivered while we were away.*

*One of my dad's first jobs was delivering milk door to door in England. He did this at a very young age in order to help with the family finances. Clearly, he wanted to instill the same sense of hard work in his three children, and was willing to support our efforts to ensure that we too understood the correlation between hard work and money. This Croxon work ethic seemed to define all three of us as we embarked on our various careers.*

• • • •

Noel saved his earnings to purchase a bike of his very own, which he diligently looked after. It did its job getting him to his work, to school, and back throughout the year. He sold chocolate bars in the school yard, too. His classmates would marvel at Noel's ability to quickly calculate the cost and change in his head. His prowess with numbers became increasingly noticeable within the classroom as well – the teacher's refrain: "Now you be quiet, Noel. Let someone else answer." But the answers were always there, waiting in his head. He also loved the forward pull of learning.

As Noel approached fourteen years of age, his formal education was coming to a close, but the love of discipline, order, and mental challenge would stick with him. Due to his exceptional performance in the school, he was selected from his class to write a school exam for a scholarship to a private school in Chelmsford. He knew he could easily pass the exam, but he declined the offer. His parents would not have been able to afford the boarding costs, so he simply told them that he would not take the entrance test. They said nothing, but seemed relieved. Noel accepted that this was the way it had to be, and did not spend a moment feeling sorry for himself.

The war dragged on and his parents decided to split up again, but Noel would not let the weight of these personal and national trials weigh him down. He repeated those words of Churchill: "Let it roll. Let it roll on full flood, inexorable, irresistible, benignant, to broader lands and better days."

It was time to move on.

A pessimist sees the difficulty
in every opportunity;

An optimist sees the opportunity
in every difficulty.

Winston Churchill

# Chapter Five

# Light at the End
# of a Dark Road

· · · · ·

Noel spent the final years of the war first living and working in Epping, then making his way to London. He had taken over Cran Jr.'s job working as a rewind-boy and cinema projectionist at the local theatre, and had even replaced him at Mrs. Miles' lodging house where he had stayed. Eighty percent of Noel's salary went to Mrs. Miles, leaving only two shillings and sixpence each week for spending. Each night after the show closed and customers left the cinema, Noel would scan the aisles to ensure that no cigarettes were left burning on the floor. He saw the opportunity this afforded, and would excitedly make his way along the rows, gathering up half-smoked cigarettes, abandoned gloves, candies, and coins.

After a year in Epping, Noel joined his mother and siblings

in Finsbury Park. He continued his work as a projectionist, first at the Marlborough, an Odeon Theatre on Holloway Road, and later transferred to the bigger and newer Astoria Theatre nearer to home. He chuckled as he leaned through the small glass window above the theatre and spied on the canoodling couples in the back rows. He also loved to see the smooth round-and-round movement of the movie projector and the astounding images it cast on the screen below: glamourous actors in cars travelling fast along cliff-side roads, actresses' hair blowing in the wind as they sailed on yachts across vast seas, scenes from all around the world. Things and places Noel had never seen in reality.

One of his responsibilities, along with the other men who worked there, was fire watching, which entailed spending the night awake at the theatre, watching and listening for the clank of incendiary bombs hitting the roof or bouncing against the walls of the building. If they had fallen, Noel and his colleagues would have had to toss down their hand of cards, spring into action and rush to put out the fires, but the theatre was spared.

Nighttime prevails in all of Noel's memories from that time, as though the sun had not risen for years. He recalls waiting up at night, at work or home, as German Doodlebugs descended over London one by one. These bombs with wings did one of two things: suddenly tilted, nosedived, and exploded, or their engines cut out and they floated down silently. Breath was held and hearts pounded loudly in that dark, quiet air, as Londoners waited for impact.

A short-lived romance invaded that time as well – walking a colleague named Betty Henry home after work and stealing kisses on the doorstep of her flat. But mostly, the time was filled with uncertainty and hunger. Rationing continued, ensuring that Noel's adolescent stomach was never full enough. While Yvonne got a job in a clothing store, Noel's mother continued working the evenings serving drinks at a bar, and spent her days caring for young Leo. She brought her work home at times, occasionally showing up at the flat with male customers.

One night seventeen-year-old Noel was jolted out of deep sleep by the blast of a doodlebug hitting a building the next street over. Glass windows shattered throughout the Croxon's house, and a split second later chunks of ceiling plaster fell to the floor. Noel burst from his bed, put on his shoes, and joined his brothers and mother in the hallway. Without speaking a word to one another, they all set to work. Noel found the broom and dustpan and began to sweep up the debris, the crunch of glass beneath his feet. This was the way at that time: everyone had to simply carry on.

Sometimes the nights were opaque with the thick fog caused by coal fire heating. People wandered, blind, along streets, not sure of where they were; handkerchiefs were dotted with black substance, buses were led by a curbside conductor who held flares in his hand to guide the vehicles. It was much like a bad dream from which the nation could not awaken.

And then they did.

The levity of May 8th, 1945, was a welcome change from the cautiousness of the previous years. Noel and Cran Jr. pressed their way through the throngs of people. Noel held onto the back of his brother's coat to avoid being engulfed by the bouncing crowd. A brass band played somewhere beyond the chaos of the Mall, but the dancing revellers didn't need any music to bolster their frenetic merry-making. The war was over. Winston Churchill had proclaimed this day as Victory in Europe Day (VE Day), a holiday for the nation. It seemed that everyone had made their way to Buckingham Palace to engage in rowdy celebration of a peaceful future. Young couples kissed, a soldier sat precariously atop a lamppost waving the Union Jack, people formed conga lines or splashed through fountains, and those in uniform bounced higher than the rest. There was laughter and song everywhere. Noel smiled at an elderly couple, twirling beneath the dark clouds.

A hush fell over the crowd as figures emerged onto the balcony of the Palace. It was the grinning Prime Minister, hands held behind his back, flanked by the King, Queen, and their two daughters. The royals raised their arms, bent at ninety degrees, and performed their regal wave. A deafening roar swept through the masses.

Cran Jr. and Noel passed numerous public houses on their way to the Palace that night, each pub crammed to bursting with celebrants. Queues snaked through the narrow streets. Seventeen-year-old Noel was hugged by a stranger, and a frothy pint of ale was thrust into his hand.

A weight lifted from the nation, the world. The thick tension of the previous years had become so normal that up until VE Day, people could no longer sense how it slowed and fatigued them, how it kept their ears glued to the radio and eyes fixed on the evening sky. Now their brows smoothed, hips moved, lips kissed, chins lifted, and feet danced. Women tore down their mandatory blackout curtains and sewed themselves long skirts, which they twirled late into the night. Others tossed those dark cloths into raging bonfires, around which they sang. The city streets that had been shrouded through wartime nights were now flooded with light.

With VE Day, the nation woke up. Children's laughter filled the bomb sites where they tossed bricks, made games out of rubble, and played cricket. Life would finally go on.

Chapter Six

# PO/X 125523

· · · · ·

Spring turned to summer, summer to autumn, autumn to winter. Christmas, also Noel's eighteenth birthday, approached. The weather turned wet and cool, the fog returned, and Noel prepared for conscription.

Cran's Jr.'s weak knees, operated on when he was a child, disqualified him from entering the armed forces. Noel, on the other hand, passed the medical and awaited his orders, which came in March 1946. He was sent a ticket and instructions to report three days later to the Royal Marine barracks in the town of Deal, Kent.

Noel pressed his few possessions into a small suitcase. He said goodbye to his cinema colleagues and family and made his way to the Charing Cross railroad station. Alone in the train car, Noel enjoyed the powerful forward push of the locomotive through the heavy grey world outside the window. He passed several sites covered in rubble, and others that had already been cleaned up following the war.

When Noel arrived in Kent, he disembarked and noticed five other boys descending from the train onto the platform, holding baggage, and clutching a paper much like the one Noel had received by mail. They must all have December birthdays like me, he thought, aware that the timing of being called into National Service was based on date of birth. Sidling over to the group, Noel suspected these might be his companions for the next eighteen months.

"Hello, I'm Noel Croxon," he said to one slight fellow in an oversized overcoat.

"I'm Noel Flynn," said the young man, likely also a Christmas baby. Noel smiled.

A Marine sergeant appeared in a burst of heavy footsteps and sharp motions, and the six young conscripts were led off swiftly to their temporary lodgings, a converted church filled with rows of bunks. Somehow, as Noel was led to his bed, he felt very little concern about his new occupation and simply went with the flow. The next day, the forty-two-member Squad 925 was directed to the clothing department and dressed with Royal Marine clothing – everything from socks to berets. Noel was assigned his number, PO/X 125523. He was determined to do things right. He got his hair cut to specifications, ensuring the mandated two-inch space between the top of his ears and the beret did not have hair long enough to be "grab-able." The squad members were given empty packages in which to place their civilian clothes for sending home. Some of the men crammed large bundles into their boxes, but Noel folded the trousers and shirt he came in, and placed them in the box for posting.

The highlight of the day came when each squad member was each issued his own Lee Enfield rifle. Noel carefully examined the shining wood of his weapon. Over the next months, the gun would become Noel's almost constant companion as he learned to care for it, clean it, shoot it, march with it, and perform drills with it.

Within a week, the squad was moved into their barracks for their three-month stay. Noel organized his uniform on the hangers at the foot of his bunk bed. He adapted quickly to the orderliness of life in the marines. Each morning, he got up early to ensure he was properly dressed, boots polished, and ready for daily examination by the sergeant. During the day, the squad was taught to assemble in lines. At first, the forty-two young lads jostled violently for their spots, but soon learned to sort themselves neatly into three lines. They were schooled in the precise art of saluting and standing at attention, as well as every pace of the march. They were led out on long treks across the countryside in sunshine and rain.

In the gymnasium, Noel felt his scrawny frame thicken with muscles as he followed the exhausting regimen of pull-ups, push-ups, and running. At the end of only two months in Deal, he had put four inches on his chest.

Seeds of confidence began to germinate in those months as well. Noel was asked to take his third-class certificate of education, and passed it with ease.

After three months of this basic training and a week of leave, the squad packed their meagre military belongings and moved west to Lymstone. Noel had never ventured so far in his life and the moors of Devonshire seemed like the edge of the earth. He launched himself into training, which had been diversified beyond sheer discipline and stamina, to include field craft, use of platoon weaponry, map-reading, and rifle range shooting. The squad spent cold unhappy nights camping out on the moors, shivering beneath the rain and clouds.

One afternoon, Noel was taking a break after a two-hour shift guarding the camp's gate. He heard the sound of gun shots in the distance and walked out to the rifle range to investigate. Five squad members were engaged in a target-shooting contest. One of them had placed a hat on the ground, in which a few pennies were scattered. The individual with the most bulls-eyes would win. The fellows invited Noel to join them, and he eagerly accepted the challenge, hoping his rifle training would prove worthwhile. They cleared a way. Noel loaded and lifted his weapon, squinting at the target in the distance. An icy breeze blew, but Noel did not feel it. He found his steady position, pulled the butt of the rifle into the pocket of his shoulder, dropped his cheek, and aligned the rifle sight. Holding his breath, he pressed and released the trigger. Bang! A bulls-eye! Noel grinned widely and the group of young men erupted in applause. This became

Noel's favourite past-time, both because he excelled at it and because he often won the pennies.

As the basic training was coming to a close, many squad members declared that they would be continuing on to become Commandos. Noel did not relish the idea of more severe physical training so he sought out other options and found that becoming a cook was the only other position available to him. Nonetheless, he applied and waited for the reply. Before it came, he was asked to participate in an interview process with two other men from the squad. They had been specially chosen to take on a role that required them to engage in intense rifle training and then return to camp to teach what they learned to a new squad. Noel was surprised he had been selected as he was not the most physically fit among his squad. The small seeds of confidence planted earlier continued to grow.

Noel was relocated to a camp in Browndown, Hampshire. During his six weeks there, he put his proficiency for intense focus to work. He spent hours studying the weapons and perfecting his skills at target practice. When he returned to the old training ground in Devon, he stood a little taller. He was assigned a squad, and was promoted to the rank of Corporal. Immediately, he began teaching and delighted in passing along his newly-acquired knowledge.

## Sheilagh's Kitchen. February 4, 2017

*Out of the blue, Noel produces an old black and white photograph from his wallet, and asks Claire to identify the statue featured in it. His mouth curls up into a smile as he waits for her answer, and when she is unable to produce one, his grin turns to a delighted smile as he explains that it's the mermaid statue in Copenhagen Harbour, modelled after the character from the Hans Christian Andersen fairytale. Observing this exchange, I am struck by the sudden memory of a dinner-time family ritual from when I was growing up. Noel would conduct something we called "Question Period," which entailed him quizzing us on arithmetic, geography, or general knowledge. Bruce, Michael, and I would compete to be the first to answer, and if we responded correctly, we received a quarter. I did my best to show up my brothers, and fortunately, I seemed to have inherited Noel's memory for facts and figures.*

During training one day, Noel climbed into a trench in order to demonstrate to his squad how to fire an anti-tank gun, called a P.I.A.T. As the rain began to pour down, the men leaned forward to listen closely to Noel's instructions. Noel showed them how to plant their feet and hold the weapon. The ground was slippery with mud, but Noel continued with the demonstration. As he released the trigger, something he had done hundreds of times before, his feet swept out from beneath him. The weapon recoiled, smashing him in the upper jaw as he fell to the wet earth. He looked up, embarrassed, at the concerned faces of young men. His mouth filled with blood and broken teeth, his ego bruised.

At the infirmary, four of Noel's teeth were removed and he was fitted for a denture. For several weeks, while he awaited his denture, he instructed the squad without his front teeth. He imagined them snickering at the memory of his muddy fall, but he pushed aside that thought as much as he could and pressed on.

Only months later, Noel's National Service came to its formal end. Released from his duties, he returned home to London, where so much of the damage left by the Blitz had been cleaned up, and plans for rebuilding established. It was as though, like Noel had, London awaited dentures to fill its gaping holes.

With all of the experiences of the last eighteen months tucked up inside him, Noel returned to his role at the same cinema.

Day after day, he arrived at work and played and replayed the same films. Snuck in games of cards with the same colleagues. Peered through the glass down at the same couples snuggling in the back rows. Watched the same scenes, same actors' faces flicker across the screen, and felt the weight of a stationary life. His time in the marines, meeting new people, learning new skills, and marching across new landscapes rendered him more restless than ever.

One morning Noel woke up and decided he did not want to be stuck on replay anymore. The clock was ticking loudly in his ears, and it was time to listen to it.

Striving for success without hard work
is like trying to harvest where you haven't planted.

David Bly

# Chapter Seven

# A Working Man

· · · · ·

Noel was dressed in his Sunday best as he sat in a stranger's office. He had seen an ad in the paper calling for young job applicants, made an appointment, and showed up armed with the hope that his promotion in the Marines stood him in good stead for a new and better job. As he shifted in a wooden chair across the desk from this man, Noel was struck by the memory of the woman in the food shop in Ongar, who had beckoned him in, handed him a shopping list and offered him the role of errand boy. That had been his first job. He was as eager today as he had been those many years ago.

The man behind the desk asked a series of questions about Noel's skills, and before long they both agreed that work in an office where he could put his mathematic prowess to good use would be the right place to start. The man rifled through stacks of paper and unearthed the name and number of a company seeking an assistant for their chief cashier. Waving the precious information in the air, the man dialed a clothing retail chain called Hope Brothers and let them know that Noel would be on his way over. The sound of the telephone clicking into its bed was reminiscent of the Ongar shop door clicking shut when Noel had set out on his first errands.

The Hope Brothers head office was in Ludgate Hill, just down the road from Saint Paul's Cathedral. Noel took a deep breath before walking up the main steps and entering the building. The office was a mess of desks, paper piles, and leather-bound binders. There was the noise of a typewriter, and a lingering haze of grey-blue cigarette smoke.

Noel began his position immediately, taking on the responsibility of paying all the bills and making all the deposits, which consisted of gathering up the money midday, and walking the mile to the local bank with it all tucked into a fabric bag. There would be one hundred pounds or more in the sack, depending on the day. Somehow, the potential risks of this daily excursion never occurred to him, and, luckily, trouble never found him. He simply travelled to and from the bank enjoying the chance to be on the move.

Day after day, Noel worked away diligently in the office, perched on the edge of his stool at a high table. By early afternoon on most days he could overhear the rhythmic deep breaths of his overweight boss, snoozing at his desk just a few feet away. This kind of laziness irritated Noel, so he would do his best to narrow his focus and finish his work swiftly. Often, he crept about the office seeking productive ways to pass the rest of the work day, sometimes  tidying up files or flipping through log books. Sometimes there  was simply nothing left to do. On those days, he had no choice but to be still, and dwell angrily on how much time was being wasted and how much more efficiently things could be run.

Noel could sense that his numerical skills were valuable at the office, and wanted to deepen them. He registered for a night school bookkeeping course, easily picking up the lessons and completing the work. On examination night, he breezed through the test, checked his responses twice and stood to leave the examination room. The invigilator stood up and strongly urged Noel to check over the exam once more. Obediently, Noel sat down and looked it over again, making no changes, then waited for the clock to run out. A few weeks later, the final results were released, Noel learned that he had passed with honours. Little by little, these small triumphs were building his self-confidence.

Thrilled by his recent successes and frustrated by the disorderliness of his current workplace, Noel answered an advertisement for an accounts receivable ledger clerk position in an automotive dealership near his London home in Highbury. He was hired on the spot, and resigned from Hope Brothers, a smile plastered upon his face. The boss responded to the resignation with a deep frown, and quickly offered Noel more money to reconsider. But Noel was already on the move. The new job was closer to home, and he could walk or bicycle there. His main reason for switching positions was to quell the dissatisfaction he had felt while wasting so much time at his old job. Time was a resource and he hated to squander it.

Noel began his new job working at the dealership on September 19, 1949, right around the time he was also learning to drive. After a near-lifetime of biking everywhere, cars were creeping into his life. He adored how, in a car, he could increase the circumference of his daily movement, travelling quickly to places farther and farther away.

The duties at his new place of employment included recording all sales transactions, whether credit sales or cash sales. The actual accounts receivable ledger was a whopping six inches thick. Noel often flipped through it, finding peace in the reliability of all the numbers lined up neatly, doing all the sums easily in his head, as there were no calculators. It did not take him long to acclimatize to the job and realize that it was not particularly challenging – he completed his work efficiently and spent a great deal of his office time looking for other work to do. He had two work colleagues, one who oversaw the accounts payable and payroll, and the other who managed the general ledger and financial statements. Both of these individuals were enrolled in correspondence accounting courses, an idea that appealed to bored Noel. He registered with the British Association of Accountants and Auditors and began studying for the course. A year later he took the intermediate exam and passed two of the six subjects (Executive Law and Accounts and Auditing) with honours. The two colleagues, who had also completed the course, resigned from their jobs, and only an assistant was hired to replace them. In addition to his own role, Noel found that he was able to manage the work of his two former colleagues as well. Since he was preparing all the month-end figures and financial statements, he was asked to report directly to the president.

It did not take long for Noel to acclimatize to the tasks and responsibility of his new role. Again, he found he was done his daily work quite quickly. One afternoon, he closed his ledger and stalked the office for extra tasks. The president saw Noel stacking some papers on shelves outside his office, and called him inside.

"Croxon, if you're so eager to find something to do," he said with a grin, "re-open the audited books and figure out why the sales ledgers for the year were one shilling off." He gestured towards four extremely large leather-bound books and added, "Good luck!"

Surely the president knew this was a near impossible challenge, but Noel was determined to succeed. He lugged the giant texts over to his desk and sat down. After a few minutes of staring at the mountainous pile and wondering how to go about the task, he decided that all he needed to do was begin at the beginning and move through, line-by-line, tracking forward through the pages naturally and consistently, like the comforting forward movement of a car on the open road. He picked up the first ledger and flipped it open. In his head he began the sums. At the bottom of the first column on the first page, he stopped. It was two shillings out. A surge of adrenaline coursed through his body. He continued onto the next page and it was one shilling out. Voila! He solved the problem in the first two pages. The miraculous nature of his quick discovery baffled Noel. He was prepared for logic, but wasn't used to luck. Still scratching his head, he walked back into the president's office and declared his successful completion of the challenge.

The self-assuredness that enveloped Noel as he busily pored over numbers and business statements seemed to ebb away in the world outside the office. As he put on his coat at the end of the day, he stood tall and energetic, but his gait slowed and his body lowered to a stoop with each step away from work. Seeing his friends paired off in couples, he mustered the courage to ask a young lady named Beatrice (Betty) Moyle out on a date, and although their dating evolved quickly into an engagement and marriage under a year later, Noel remained tentative in her presence. After their wedding in May 1950, they moved into a small rented flat, which was the top floor of a house. They both spent most of their time at their respective jobs and very little time together. After two years of marriage, Noel began to notice how Betty was coming home later and later from work, withdrawn and tired.

One cloudy evening Noel returned home from work, opened up the flat door and hung up his umbrella. Betty's coat was not there, but he figured she was likely late at work as usual. He shuffled around the kitchen in the hopes of finding something appetizing to eat. He had not yet noticed the white folded paper adorned with his handwritten name, waiting on the centre of the table. He filled the kettle and sat down. Finally spotting the note, he snatched it and opened it up. The next moments were a swell of senses: the sudden tightening of the throat, a wave of nausea, a memory of his mother's back as she walked away into a field, the blur of the black writing, the endless scream of the kettle. Betty had left Noel for another man. The luck of that day with the ledgers seemed so far away.

1953 was a year enshrouded with regret, self-doubt, and an incessant need to work. Noel felt antsy. He was eager to improve his working position and boost his bruised self-esteem. An advertisement for an automobile accountant position in Nairobi, Kenya, caught his eye. He responded and was offered the role. The draw of a life in that faraway land tempted him, but something held him back. Perhaps it was the unsatisfactory remuneration, or perhaps it was the young woman he had just met.

Noel had first seen Norma Hudson Gilpin ironing clothes in the hallway of the house where he had a flat. She was staying with friends in the neighbouring unit. Her head was bowed solemnly as she pressed down on her nurse's uniform. Although she was quite petite, there was something independent and grand about her stance, something determined in the way she moved along the shortest line from the board to the door, something focused about the force of her weight on the iron. Often Noel leaned against the wall and struck up conversation with her, enjoying her stories of life as a nurse-in-training, admiring her dark hair, her smooth golden-brown skin. It took a while for Noel to gather up the courage to ask this new friend out on a date, but eventually he did. They enjoyed each other's company, and shared a mutual love of travel, although Norma's travel had been far more extensive than Noel's at that point.

They planned a dream holiday together. First they went to Copenhagen, then on to Oslo, where they stayed with Noel's sister, Yvonne. She had married Anton, a Norwegian airman, and moved to Norway following the war. They had three children at that time, Diana who had been born in England, and Astri and Ragnar who were born in Norway. Norma and Noel spent a memorable week there before they boarded the ship in Oslo to head back to Britain.

Now that Noel had seen more of the world, London seemed somehow too small and familiar upon his return. He continued at his job while Norma resumed her training in midwifery in Oxford and Worcester. They managed to see each other from time to time, until Norma announced she would be going home to Jamaica. Noel sent her off, promises of a pen-pal-ship lingering in the air, and she was gone. Noel imagined Norma on the long voyage across the Atlantic, the black ocean waters disappearing beneath the ship, new lands and experiences beyond the horizon.

They kept in touch, mostly exchanging postcards with scenes from local excursions and long letters detailing the events of their lives and their future plans. Norma's clear intentions were to immigrate to Canada, so she successfully pursued a job at the Toronto Western Hospital, and finally moved there in 1955. The thoughts of Norma and the strange new land across the sea lured Noel. The postcards from Canada showed the dramatic change of seasons, each of which was a bold exclamation of the circular movement of time. Noel longed to see these endless forests of bright leaves in fall and thick beds of snow in winter. In March 1956, he quit his job and booked his passage to Canada. His eyes and mind were fixed on getting to this new home. He travelled out of Southampton on the Cunard H. M. S. Ascania. As the ship left the harbour, he stood on deck, nodded one final goodbye to his homeland, and then turned his face to the open water ahead.

R.M.S Ascania
Departed Southhampton
March 16, 1956

From left: Leo, Noel, Cran Jr., Cran Sr., Jo and Yvonne
outside their family home 1940

Marine Unit in Training
Corporal Noel Croxon far left

Noel
1943

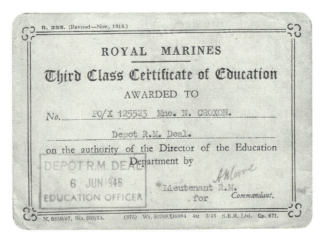

Certificate of Education from the Royal Marines
June 1946

# ROYAL SOCIETY FOR THE ENCOURAGEMENT
# OF ARTS, MANUFACTURES AND COMMERCE
# LONDON

COMMERCIAL EXAMINATIONS—ELEMENTARY STAGE

*Noel Croxon*

of the Crouch End Evening Institute,

having undergone the Examination prescribed by the Royal Society for the
Encouragement of Arts, Manufactures and Commerce, in the year 1949, has been
granted by The Council of the Society, on the award of their Examiner

THIS CERTIFICATE WITH CREDIT IN

## BOOK-KEEPING

Given under our hands

Chairman of the Local Committee

Signature of the holder of this Certificate

Chairman of the Council of the
Royal Society of Arts

Secretary of the Royal Society of Arts

*.* The Examinations comprise an Advanced and Intermediate Stage (Classes 1 and 2) and an Elementary Stage (Pass with Credit and Pass)

Bookkeeping Certificate
1949

D.L.28 (c)

**DRIVING TEST**

Ref. No. _____ 400840 C _____
(To be quoted in all correspondence)

Tel. No. Abbey 4333. Ext. _____ 4·5 _____

Date as
Postmark

1. The receipt of your remittance value :—
   Ten shillings. 10/-
   Two shillings and sixpence. 2/6 } is acknowledged.

2. Arrangements have been made for you to be tested on _____ MON. 5ᵗʰ July, 19 54 , at 2·15 p.m. ,

   at _____ AVENUE LODGE, PARK AVENUE, WOOD GREEN,

3. **THIS IS THE EARLIEST DATE THAT CAN BE OFFERED. PLEASE DO NOT WRITE OR TELEPHONE FOR AN EARLIER APPOINTMENT. IF IT IS IMPOSSIBLE TO ATTEND PLEASE QUOTE THE ABOVE REF. NO. AND DATE AND PLACE OF THE APPOINTMENT OFFERED; THE NEXT AVAILABLE DATE WILL THEN BE SUBSTITUTED. FAILURE TO ATTEND WITHOUT PRIOR NOTIFICATION MAY LEAD TO A LONG WAIT FOR ANOTHER APPOINTMENT.**

4. (a) You must provide a suitable vehicle bearing a current Licence.

   (b) You must be covered against Third Party Risks.

5. If you have a Provisional Licence, the vehicle must carry "L" plates.

6. PLEASE BE PUNCTUAL.

7. You should bring with you this card together with your current Driving Licence and Insurance Certificate. (Note : If either is out of date, even by one day, the test cannot be conducted.)

8. In the case of Fog, Ice, or Snow please telephone.

Remarks :—

Wt. 26962/7995 100m 10/53—McC & Co Ltd—R 186 (667)

**ON HER MAJESTY'S SERVICE**

LONDON, S.W.
11 M
1954
H

BRITISH INDUSTRIES
3 – 14
LONDON & ?

OFFICIAL
PAID

Mʳ N. Croxon

18 Mountview Road

N.4

please return to :—
to the Licensing Authority,
...olitan Traffic Area,
...ney House,
Marsham Street,
London, S.W.1.

Driving Test Confirmation
1954

# The British Association of Accountants and Auditors

LIMITED (BY GUARANTEE)

(Incorporated 5th September 1923)

## This is to Certify that

Noel Croxon

of

London

## has PASSED the

Intermediate Examination

in accordance with the Bye-Laws of the above

Association, with Credit in the subjects of Executorship
Law & Accounts and Auditing.

Given under our hands at London, this
Twentieth day of January One thousand
nine hundred and fifty six.

_____ Chairman.

_____ Member of Council.

_____ Secretary.

*This Certificate does not constitute membership of the Association.*

686

Accounting Certificate
1956

Consciousness is only possible through change;
change is only possible through movement.

Aldous Huxley

# PART TWO

·····

## Picking up Speed

Continuous effort - not strength or intelligence -
is the key to unlocking our potential.

Winston Churchill

Chapter Eight

# Passage to a New World
· · · · ·

It was Noel's first time on a ship, and he loved to be on deck, feel the ocean breeze on his face, and stare overboard at the undulating, dark water. The sailing was smooth on the first day as they travelled to Cherbourg to collect more passengers before continuing along the English Channel. Everyone stood gathered against the railings, chatting happily. By the second night, the ship was already well out in the open sea, where it was pitched and tossed by massive waves. One by one the passengers turned shades of green and rushed to their cabins. Feeling extremely well, Noel arrived at the dining hall and found he was alone at an eight-person table; the rest of the room was nearly empty. He ate quietly, watching the water in his glass swoosh from side to side. The next day, to occupy his time, he attempted to play cards, but they fell off the table with each violent movement of the vessel. He wandered the empty decks alone, and stood a long while at the stern. He was transfixed by the sight of the rear propeller as it rose above the surface and then submerged again. The ship made two distinct sounds: a whirring as the propeller came up one side of the wave and pushed air or the roar of moving water as it disappeared beneath the wave. Noel returned to that spot day after day, as the poor conditions continued, and the passage was extended.

A few days later, the passengers began to emerge from their rooms, drained and hungry. As the voyage progressed, Noel met a couple of people, and enjoyed talking with them about what awaited them on the west side of the Atlantic. The eleventh day was sunny and the waters were finally calm. People pointed off into the distance, sure it was land they could see on the horizon. As the day wore on, New York rose out of the sea before them, and there were ecstatic shouts from eager passengers. They passed below the Statue of Liberty, and some of the travellers waved at her expectantly.

After disembarking, waiting in long lines, and showing his visa, Noel made his way to Central Station. On the street outside, he gazed at the impossible upward stretch of skyscrapers. The train took him from that noisy place, out along the edge of highways, across wide empty fields, and finally across the border at Niagara Falls where he became a landed immigrant. It was April 2, 1956. Noel had no clue what the future would hold for him as he continued on a train along the shores of Lake

Ontario. He dreamed of beautiful Norma and the possibilities contained within a new city, a new land. England, the war, and heartache seemed a lifetime ago already.

Noel's journey ended and began anew at Union Station in Toronto. As he left the train, with ninety-two dollars in his pocket, there was Norma, dressed neatly and waiting on the platform, a subtle smile on her face. Ever practical, she worried that he had not eaten properly and escorted him across the street where they ate breakfast and caught up on their news. Everything was set up for Noel. Norma had arranged for him to share a room rental at 173 Roxborough Street with another fellow named Sean Duffy. The accommodation was reasonably priced, ten dollars and fifty-cents a week, plus fifteen cents a day for coffee and toast, and another fifty cents for eggs and bacon at dinnertime. Noel appreciated that Norma lived nearby with two other girls.

Now that he was reunited with Norma, the first order of business was to find a suitable career. Never one to procrastinate, Noel launched his job search almost immediately. He would have begun the day he arrived, but it was Easter Monday and he had erroneously assumed that Canadians took that day as a holiday just as Britons do. The first thing the day after his arrival, he set about responding to ads in the newspaper. After making a few calls, he had interviews arranged for that very day, as well as for the following two days.

The meetings went well, and he left each one with a job offer. On Friday morning, Noel picked up the paper and saw that a car dealership called Robertson Motors was seeking an office manager. It felt like the right opportunity. Without even calling first, he took the streetcar out to their premises at Danforth and Coxwell and boldly asked to see Ivan Ferguson, the man whose name was listed in the advertisement. Mr. Ferguson shuffled out of his office, barely looked at Noel and grunted, "I'm busy. Come back later."

Noel turned on his heels, travelled back to his flat in a huff, and contemplated not returning to the dealership. For a long while, he lay on his bed, staring at the ceiling. Then the thought struck him: What have I got to lose? It would only cost him a couple hours and a nickel on the streetcar. He stood, washed his face, and prepared to return.

That afternoon at the dealership Noel was interviewed by three different people: Grover Robertson, Ivan, and Harold Dessen, a chartered accountant. At the end of the discussions, Ivan offered Noel a job starting at seventy dollars a week. With a small surge of confidence, Noel called the places where he had been offered a job on Tuesday, Wednesday, and Thursday and turned them all down and accepted the role at Robertson Motors.

Noel hit the ground running at his new place of work. His job included recording the purchase and sales of all the dealership's vehicles, and producing inventory documentation. He completed these tasks quickly, and would jump up to look for extra things to do to fill the time. He would stalk the hallways in the early afternoon, stopping to ask his colleagues if they wanted help and eagerly taking on any tasks that needed doing. At the doorway of Mr. Ferguson's office, Noel would peek in regularly and see the elderly man snoring away in his plump chair.

Robertson Motors also had a car leasing company, which was a new business at that time. The dealership asked Noel if he would take on the accounting for the leasing company. He happily accepted and was paid thirty-five dollars a month for this new work. Often, Noel would lug work documentation home on public transit, spreading his paperwork across the seats. As his streetcar rattled its way down the Danforth, Noel would focus on his figures, occasionally glancing up to see the scenes of his new city out the side windows. This new land seemed full of promise.

There is no doubt that it is around the family
and the home that all the greatest virtues,
the most dominating virtues of human society,
are created, strengthened and maintained.

Winston Churchill

# Chapter Nine

# Family Ties

· · · · ·

To Noel, marriage seemed like the natural next step in his relationship with Norma. Even with the painful recollection of his parents' tumultuous marriage, and the haunting memory of Betty's handwritten goodbye note, Noel and Norma began to talk about setting a wedding date. They had been diligently putting away funds, but hadn't managed to save enough for both a wedding reception and a honeymoon.

"I'll ask my mother for a loan," suggested Norma.

It took Noel some time to warm up to the idea. He was not accustomed to asking family for help; even if he had, his family members wouldn't have had any extra funds to offer. It wasn't a matter of pride, he had simply become used to fending for himself. Besides, he had not even met his soon-to-be in-laws.

But strong-willed Norma was firm and insisted on this course of action and Noel was forced to relent. Norma's mother lent them four hundred dollars. Added to their own savings, the money was enough to pull together a small reception at the Old Mill in the west end of Toronto. They were wed on September 15, 1956. The newlyweds drove eastward and spent a week honeymooning in the Laurentians, north of Montreal.

After their time away, they returned to a newly furnished apartment rental at 1545 Bathurst Street. While they were pleased to have a place to call their own, Noel's daily commute to Robertson Motors was lengthened. He had to take a streetcar, then a subway, and then a second streetcar, but he used the time well, bringing more and more work home each evening.

As the couple settled into domestic life, Noel became increasingly troubled at work. He was certain he could excel in the role of secretary-treasurer without any problems. In a bold move, Noel applied for that role with a Ford dealer in Weston, Toronto, and was offered the job. It would be a hefty increase in salary to one hundred dollars a week, plus a new car! Noel returned to Robertson's with the news of his offer, and they agreed to match it. In addition, the dealership promised Noel that he would become secretary-treasurer once Ivan Ferguson retired in a few months. Noel opted to stay.

Norma and Noel saved all the money Norma earned, and lived on Noel's salary alone. Their relationship was defined by order and pragmatism. They both cherished frugality and bought nothing beyond what they needed and could afford. Adding to her busy nurse's schedule, Norma began to sell Avon Products to her hospital colleagues. The couple monitored their savings and spoke practically about using them to make a down payment on a house where they could start a family.

Two years of marriage had passed by and still Noel had not met Norma's family. They made plans to visit Jamaica over Christmas in 1958 to see her parents, brother, and sister. As it was his first flight, Noel took note of every detail of the air travel experience – the noisy propeller plane, the stops to refuel along the way, the fierce vibration of the aircraft, and the bird's-eye view of Jamaica's rich turquoise waters and lush green hills.

Norma's mother Cynthia, father Jigs, brother Deryck, and sister Phyllis greeted them at the airport. Noel quickly developed an affection for this new land, its vibrant colours, delicious food, and endless sunshine. He marvelled at the Gilpins' fine manners and well-run household with a maid, cook, and other servants. He was not used to such lavish living. He was much less enthused, however, about spending his nights sleeping under a mosquito net.

One day over breakfast Deryck mentioned that he had recently obtained his driving learner's permit. Noel gulped down his coffee, stood up, and announced, "Well then, we're going for a drive."

The two men climbed into the car and ventured out onto the rough country roads for hours of driving practice. Noel took this teaching time very seriously, carefully explaining the rules of the road, providing advice and encouragement, and rolling down the windows to feel the wind in his hair. Deryck seemed to share this love of the open road.

••••

**Deryck Gilpin.**
**Get Back Behind the Wheel.**

*I've known Noel for over fifty-five years, as a friend, teacher, boss, partner, and confidante.*

*Some very early memories of our relationship stand out to me.*

*I first met Noel when he visited Jamaica with Norma. I was sixteen and had just obtained my learner's permit. Noel decided that he would brave the treacherous roads with me at the wheel. Driving up one steep, winding, and wet road, we encountered a speeding cyclist coming down the road on our side. He couldn't stop nor completely avoid the car, but managed to sacrifice the bike and narrowly avoid the wheels himself. Thankfully, the cyclist was not injured, except for some scrapes, and walked away carrying his completely destroyed bicycle.*

*I was pretty shaken up. Noel, on the other hand, seemed unperturbed. He insisted I get back behind the wheel, and had me drive to the local police station where we reported the incident.*

*To an impressionable teenager, Noel seemed like one really cool guy.*

*At that time, I could not have known that Noel would continue to be a guiding force in my life.*

*He helped me get my start in the auto business, offered me a partnership opportunity, and has truly been the best mentor and friend imaginable.*

••••

Back home in Toronto, Norma and Noel returned to their daily routine of work, economizing, and preparing for the next stage of their life together. In 1959, Norma became pregnant, but had an early miscarriage. In 1960, she became pregnant again. As her belly grew, so did the couple's eagerness to find a home of their own. They dreamed about finding a place close to downtown, but deemed it unreasonable as it would entail taking on two mortgages. Such an extravagance did not sit well with either of them. Instead, they sought out a home in the affordable Scarborough area, and eventually purchased a house on Neapolitan Drive. They paid seventeen-thousand and two-hundred dollars for a small three-bedroom abode, proudly offering their hard-earned savings of four-thousand and two-hundred dollars as down payment and soon moved in.

In newly-shined shoes, Noel kicked at the gravel driveway of his new house, remembering how he had played barefoot in the dirt outside his many childhood homes. He reflected on the contrast between this spacious bungalow and his father's caravan, and was grateful. His first changes to the house would be to pave over the unfinished drive, and switch the single pane windows for double glazed ones. There would be no cold draughts in his children's home. As he planned the landscaping, strategizing over where to plant hedges and gardens, he remembered how his father tended to the rows of vegetables with meticulous care.

It was not long before Bruce was born. On the evening of October 27, 1960, Norma felt her first pangs of labour. Calmly,

Noel drove her to the Toronto Western Hospital, stopping halfway to fill up the tank, much to Norma's great irritation. As was the custom in those days, Noel did not stay in the ward to await the birth of his child. Rather, he helped Norma into the hospital, returned home to sleep, and was awakened the next morning by a phone call letting him know that his son, Bruce, was born. Noel sped back to see his firstborn. As he held the healthy, sleeping baby tenderly in his arms, he felt a surge of protectiveness and an overwhelming hope for the future.

Those early days of family life passed quickly and happily. Noel loved the sense of responsibility that came with providing for a young family. In the summer of 1962, he was thrilled to learn that Norma was pregnant again. Just as his new plants were thickening and filling the garden beds, so was his family blossoming. They rejoiced again at the arrival of their daughter, Sheilagh, on February 25, 1963. There was a brief moment of worry immediately after her birth: Norma's blood was RH Negative and the infant required an immediate transfusion. Despite this challenge, Sheilagh thrived, and their home was filled with the busy sounds of a young family.

A few months later, Deryck immigrated to Canada and the family welcomed yet another member to Neopolitan Drive. The household was bursting with firsts. Deryck set about finding a job, but was turned away numerous times. Finally, after a long search he obtained a role working nights checking punch-cards at a bank. Later, he took a position with an accountant who managed small business accounts. The individual he worked for hired and fired people with regularity, but Deryck did an exceptional job and held on to the role for a long time.

The family circle continued to grow. On April 4, 1963, Noel's brother, Leo, and mother arrived in Canada. Jo went directly to Montreal to stay with her daughter, Yvonne, who now lived there. Leo came to Toronto. Noel picked him up at Pearson Airport and took him home to stay in the bustling bungalow. Fortunately, Leo quickly found a job in Brampton and went to live there just a few weeks after his arrival in Canada.

On December 14, 1964 Noel and Norma welcomed their son, Michael, into the world. Due to Norma's RH negative blood type the pregnancy had been considered high risk. Michael was induced a month early and required two blood transfusions at birth.

The house had become quite crowded, so Deryck decided to move into a house on Eglinton Avenue with some friends.

It was now just Noel's family of five in their lovely bungalow with the paved drive and flourishing garden.

All of these changes made Noel itch to move again. He and Norma found a house on Regency Square in Guildwood Village – a much more spacious home, on a corner lot, with a well-kept garden and a lush green lawn. It was a lifetime away from the cramped shadowy setting of his childhood. They sold their Neopolitan Drive abode for twenty-one thousand dollars, paid twenty-seven thousand for the new family home, and took possession in 1965. The couple joined the local golf club, inspiring a lifelong appreciation for the game.

## Sheilagh's Kitchen. June 15, 2017

*In the midst of our discussion, Noel is struck by a memory of his first trip back to England. He astounds us with his recall of details. Noel and Norma had departed from Toronto on April 4, 1967, the same day he had to complete the month-end books and send financial reports to General Motors. He was in a time crunch, so he had asked one of the office employees to come in on Saturday, April 1, her regular day off, to help complete the work. While sitting at his desk immersed in the financial statements, Noel responded to a phone call. It was the office employee who was supposed to come to help. She claimed that she was just too sick. Noel said he understood and hung up the phone. He placed his head in his hands, wondering how he would ever complete what needed to be done without the extra assistance. Moments later that same employee appeared at the door, and said, "April Fools!"*

*During the trip, Norma and Noel visited many of Noel's childhood haunts, including the town of North Weald. The shop where young Noel had purchased things when running errands for his mother had since been sold and taken over by a supermarket chain. Noel crossed over to the King's Head Pub and asked the barman whether a previous shop keeper, Mr. Waterman, still lived in town. The barman confirmed that Mr. Waterman ate his Sunday supper at the pub each week. Since it was Sunday, he suggested that Norma and Noel stay and enjoy a meal, and that he would bring Mr. Waterman over to their table when he arrived. Later, when Noel saw Mr. Waterman, he asked if he remembered him. The old man was quick to respond. "Of course, I do!" he said. "You were that little kid who would stand at the cash and add the numbers up backwards in your head faster than I could add them up looking at them in front of me."*

One night over dinner Noel looked at his wife and three small children seated around the table, and felt a wave of intense gratitude. His life had catapulted forward into a realm of safety and comfort. There was an ample selection of winter scarves and tiny mittens hung by the door. Full plates. No rabbit in sight.

Chapter Ten

# Taking Control
· · · · ·

Noel's life seemed to propel forward at an even faster pace. In addition to his usual role, he took on a side job helping the parts manager, Art Russell, set up the accounting and cash flow structure for the Canadian Tire store he was planning to open in Scarborough. During his time at Robertson's, Noel had also developed a close friendship with the business manager, Mel Smirle. In the time that Noel and Mel worked together, Mel married Sharon, they had a daughter named Sandy, and eventually bought a house across the road from the Croxon family in Guildwood Village.

Noel worked tirelessly at his Robertson Motors role, plugging away at his papers and figures, ensuring that the business accounts were orderly and up-to-date. As he sat at his desk, head down, books open, pencil and eraser poised at his fingertips, he overheard the voice of the general manager shouting grumpily over the intercom for various employees to "get the hell down here." Noel would shake his head, sigh, and continue his work.

Years earlier, Noel had heard that Alex Irvine, the highly regarded general manager of Golden Mile Motors, was soon going to be appointed as General Motors Dealer in Scarborough. One morning Noel woke up, thinking it might be nice to work with someone like Alex. Noel was not one to dwell exhaustively over decisions, and had a tendency to charge into action, so that very morning he located Alex's phone number, called him, congratulated him on his new role, and asked him who was going to be his Secretary Treasurer. Alex responded: "I'm not certain at this point, but if you would like the job, come and see me."

A few days later Noel put on his best suit, and made his way to see Alex. During the interview, Noel listened to Alex explain how he would put up twenty percent of the capital required to open the dealership, and that General Motors would cover the other eighty percent. As the major shareholder, GM would enforce certain rules and pay scales for the top employees in the dealership. As such, the secretary treasurer role would be limited to a salary of nine thousand dollars per year, the exact salary Noel was already receiving at Robertson Motors. It took less than a minute for Noel to consider the potential role. As they stood to shake hands and part ways, Noel announced confidently that he would take the job.

The difficult part was yet to come. Noel had to inform Grover Robertson that he was leaving the company with thirty days' notice. As he entered his boss's office, Noel cleared his throat and stood tall. Grover was hunched over a document, breathing heavily. He kept his focus on the page, waved Noel inside, and grunted towards a chair.

"Croxon. Nice weather today," Grover said, not looking up.

"I am taking a position at Alex Irvine's new dealership," said Noel, leaping into his news. Grover's head sprang up. Noel continued without leaving space for his employer to respond: "They've offered me nine thousand a year."

Grover's face squeezed into a scowl. After a moment of silence, he spoke up. "I'll give you sixteen-thousand if you stay here. We need you."

Noel did not need to think it over. He looked the old man in the eye and said in a calm clear voice: "If I'm worth that today, surely I was worth it yesterday." With that comment, he stood and left, hands trembling.

Over the intercom two hours later Grover called Noel back into his office. This time his voice was calm, measured. Noel tapped on the office doorway. Grover smiled and stood, as Noel entered the room.

"Tell me why you're really leaving, Croxon."

Noel fixed his eyes on the stack of magazines on Grover's cabinet. He wasn't sure how best to respond. He was someone who would only speak the straight truth. It might be better to say nothing. When Grover asked the question a second time, Noel took a deep breath and answered: "I have learned a lot from you during my seven years here, and I think I can learn even more about running a dealership from Alex. And who knows, one day I might want to be a dealer myself."

It was the least offensive truth Noel could think of. He assumed that would be the end of the discussion, that he could go in peace. He was wrong.

Grover placed both of his palms on the desk, looked Noel straight in the eyes and spoke in a low, gruff voice: "What makes you think General Motors would ever give you a dealership."

That comment sent the wheels whirring inside Noel. Grover continued to speak, his tone increasingly harsh, but Noel wasn't listening anymore. He was making a mental list of the tasks that needed to be completed before he left Robertson Motors. His mind was already driving forward toward the next challenge.

In June 1963 Noel began his work with Alex at the new dealership. For many people starting with a blank slate would seem intimidating, but not for Noel. He didn't have to clean up anyone else's mess. He loved that he could establish processes and procedures, paperwork and cash-flow, in an orderly, sensible way. With a smile, he made his first entry in the general ledger: to debit cash and credit shareholders equity for both the money that GM had put forward, as well as Alex's own money. His responsibilities did not end there. He was just as involved in helping employ people throughout the dealership. He was busy from first thing in the morning until late at night, with all his various responsibilities. His feet and brain never stopped moving.

Everything went well businesswise within the dealership; new and used car sales climbed very quickly. The team was productive and established the slogan: "We are never satisfied until you are." They were profitable every month, and both GM and their subsidiary Motors Holding Corporation were thrilled with the results. As the business grew, so did Noel's self-confidence. He liked the responsibility that came with an executive leadership role, and was relieved to no longer endure the sneer of his former employer. Instead he saw new opportunities around every corner. In fact, one of the things he did was to start a car leasing division within the dealership. He personally interviewed all prospects and built the leasing numbers to about fifty cars before employing someone to take on the department. He also received permission to hire his brother-in-law, Deryck, to fill a vacancy in the dealership office, and was immediately impressed by Deryck's impressive work ethic and skill on the job. Deryck stayed for two years before taking on a secretary-treasurer role with a dealership in

Brampton. Noel was happy to see his extended family thriving in this new land. As he looked at his stable, full life with great pleasure, the pull to keep moving never disappeared. He craved new adventures,challenges, places, and ways he could make an impact.

## Sheilagh's Kitchen. September 12, 2017

---

*There is a hint of sadness in Noel's voice as he speaks to us about his father. He regrets not having done more to support him in his later years. He expresses relief that, at the very least, he was able to visit Cran in the summer of 1967. Noel's father died in a nursing home on March 17, 1968.*

*Cran's body was donated to science to further research Syringomyelia, the debilitating disease he had suffered from all his life.*

---

Trust is earned when action meets words.

Chris Butler

Chapter Eleven

# The Beauty of Hard Work
· · · · ·

It was the summer of 1968 and Alex Irvine Motors was getting very close to one hundred percent ownership, as GM had been paid off by the profit the dealership was making. Around that time, Alex suggested that Noel and another individual consider buying a dealership that was for sale in downtown Toronto. Noel did not want a partnership with the other fellow, and, truth be told, he had not even thought of becoming a dealer. Nevertheless, he agreed to take a tour of the site with the vice president of GM Canada.

Noel said very little during that visit. As they were leaving the premises, the vice president turned to him and asked: "What do you think?"

Noel did not hesitate to reply: "I'm not interested in this particular dealership."

The vice president nodded solemnly, and they continued walking in silence. Just before they parted ways Noel added, casually: "But if the dealership in North York at Yonge and Finch ever becomes available, I would be interested."

The comment seemed like wishful thinking. It came from the same place as the comment he had made to Grover Robertson years earlier, about one day owning a dealership. It didn't seem likely to happen, particularly because Noel didn't have enough capital to purchase the dealership. Nevertheless, he boldly let the idea float out there, before shaking the vice president's hand and walking on.

Noel thought nothing further about his statement. But then, just two weeks later, his phone rang. It was the same GM vice president. They had only just exchanged greetings when the man asked: "Were you really serious about North York?"

Noel barely hesitated a moment before blurting out: "Yes." Yes. It was almost that simple – breathing out one syllable that launches you in to a future of possibilities.

They arranged to meet in person at the new dealership to review the facts and figures. It was not difficult for Noel to assess that it had been a poorly-run business, but he could also see that with the right people in charge, it could be a very profitable enterprise. It was for sale for two-hundred and sixty-thousand dollars; General Motors would put in two-hundred and ten-thousand if Noel could come up with the remaining fifty-thousand. The vice president gave him some time to think about it.

Keeping with his regular pace of action, Noel spared no time in discussing the opportunity with Norma. If they decided to make the move, they would have to use the twenty thousand dollars of equity in their home and the fifteen thousand they had invested in a pension plan and the stock market. They would still be fifteen thousand dollars short. As Noel brainstormed about where they could find the missing funds, his desire to move forward with the plan intensified. Noel was not one to get stuck. He looked for solutions everywhere. He discussed the opportunity and predicament with Alex Irvine, who insisted that Noel not sell his house. "I'll sign a note for you for twenty thousand dollars at the bank," he said.

Noel shared the situation with his friend, Mel, who had risen the ranks at work and was now General Sales Manager at Robertson Motors. He also spoke with his brother-in-law, Deryck, and suggested that both Mel and Deryck put money in and come and work with him, so that when they paid off General Motors, they would form a new company and become partners. Noel was compelled by this idea of joining forces with likeminded individuals – people he knew were committed to hard work.

Happily, both men agreed to contribute funds and become partners with Noel. There was an incredible bond of trust between these three. Noel could not put anything in writing as it was not permitted to have partners when one was joined financially with GM in the dealership. It was all done on a handshake. The men committed to making all the right business moves to ensure that they become owners of the dealership as quickly as possible. With that, Noel called General Motors to inform them that his answer was yes. Another yes.

The contract and financial details were worked out, and the money was in the bank, but Noel realized he was fourteen-hundred dollars short. As he tried to figure out what to do, Noel mentioned this predicament to Alex, who immediately pulled his cheque book out of his pocket and wrote Noel a cheque. "Pay me back whenever you can," he said, and did not blink an eye as he handed it over. All of Noel's integrity and hard work, which had earned him the trust of Alex, had paid off.

Through all of these transactions Noel felt his confidence building. He consulted with close contacts and colleagues, and they all expressed a strong belief in Noel's ability to succeed. It was with the final blessing of Alex and two close friends at his side that Noel began his work at the North York location in August 1968, in the leadup to purchasing the dealership in December.

It wasn't always smooth driving. In fact, one of the first individuals Noel met at the dealership was a fellow who he had not been able to get bonded at Alex Irvine's. Noel had heard that this man was already spreading rumours around the workplace, telling all the employees that they would lose their jobs when Noel took over. When Noel confronted him about this, the man immediately resigned. Only a few months later, Noel heard that the same individual had obtained a position at Robertson Motors.

Despite that initial hiccup, Noel set to work. As soon as he took over the dealership, he launched North York Leasing, building the workforce to about fifty before employing a leasing manager. There were some other bumps along the way: the Toronto subway system was in the midst of extending to Finch Avenue, near the dealership, so there was a lot of construction in the roadway near the entrance to the lot making it difficult for customers to enter and exit. Noel positioned members of his team near the construction site and subway exit to ensure customers had access to the dealership. Right from the beginning, this particular difficulty engendered a dealership-wide attitude that any person stepping through the doors of their establishment was a serious buyer, and not just there to kick tires. Because of this, everyone who entered that place was treated with the utmost attention and care. Sales rose quickly. The new car actual sales for the year prior was about 900 cars and trucks. In Noel and his partners' first year of operation, they sold double that amount. They aimed to turn every challenge into an opportunity to improve.

The wins continued in other ways. At the General Motors new car announcement show, to which all the managers and salesmen were invited, Mel Smirle was recognized as sales manager of the year for Toronto.

• • • •

## Mel Smirle.
## True Partnership.

*I met Noel in the spring of 1962 when I was applying for position with Robertson Motors. When I was married the following October, Noel took pity on me and loaned me his demo vehicle, a 1962 Chevrolet Belair Sedan, for the wedding. I was married in Saint Catharines, and drove to Malton Airport where I left his car. Someone had stuffed the air vents with confetti, so when Noel and Harold Lesy picked up the car and turned on the air conditioning they were covered in confetti.*

*In 1966, Noel called me to tell me his neighbour was selling his house at 80 Regency Square, which I ended up buying. Now I was living as a neighbour to Noel who had, by then, changed positions and was working for Alex Irvine Motors Ltd. We would sit out on the front porch in the evening and discuss what would be possible in the future if a dealership became available.*

*Through the years, we have travelled together extensively. To this day, we spend considerable time in each other's company, whether at his Florida property or at my summer home in the Kawartha Lakes region.*

*Our friend Bob Tomlinson coined the phrase "The Romeos" for us, meaning: Retired old men eating out.*

• • • •

It took Noel, Mel, and Deryck just under three years to repay GM's investment at which time they happily formed a new company with seventy percent of the shares in Noel's name, twenty percent in Mel's name, and ten percent in Deryck's name.

In 1972, Noel was asked to join the board of the Toronto Automobile Dealers' Association (TADA), of which he later became president. And as this personal growth occurred, so did his business. With sales continuing to rise year over year, they were running out of space to adequately serve their customers. Noel, Mel, and Deryck began to look for a new location.

A Datsun dealer Noel knew was also looking for new premises and had a connection to a site of eighteen acres just north of Steeles Avenue, on which sat an old grocery store-turned-retail-company-warehouse of thirty thousand square feet. A second dealer joined in as well, and the three of them put forward an offer and purchased the property for just 2.2 million dollars, with a mortgage of two million. Immediately, they started to convert the inside of the facility to provide enough area for two new car dealerships. The Datsun dealer took over one portion, and Noel and his partners eventually received approval from GM to move the dealership into the second portion. It wasn't long before the partners who owned the other side of the building ran into financial difficulties. One asked Noel's team to buy his portion, and the other asked them to buy part of his percentage, which they did. Noel didn't want to face the same difficulties with his business, and the two million-dollar mortgage began to weigh heavily on him. Eager to take action and reduce risk, he contacted the Bank of Nova Scotia, which lent Noel the money to pay off the mortgage. The business was secure at this point and made significant profits from 1975 to 1979.

Chapter Twelve

# Friction

· · · · ·

Down the road from Noel's location was another General Motors dealership owned by Roy Foss, who had the franchise for Pontiac and Buick. Because Foss had limited space on his premises, he met with Noel to inquire about what Noel was doing with the additional square footage on his lot and to discuss growing the dealership together. Noel's team made an agreement with Foss to develop the land into an Auto Centre. The other individual who owned the twenty-five percent of Noel's property agreed to sell it, and Noel also sold a portion of shares to Foss. Noel's team still owned their fifty. They moved forward with architects and developers to plan the centre, putting in their own sewers and turning the grasslands into roads and a paved lot. They built two new large dealerships, each approximately forty-five thousand feet, and moved into them in July 1980 with a ribbon-cutting ceremony and celebration.

Then came the growing pains. Noel's team had extended themselves financially and interest rates had begun to climb. As they had borrowed ten million dollars to do the project, Foss and Noel's dealerships had to pay very high interest rates to the bank. Sales were low mainly due to the economic climate of the time, resulting in many sleepless nights for Noel. He would often lay awake and console himself by repeatedly asking the same question: "What is the worst thing that can happen?" If he went bankrupt he knew he could start over again.

• • • •

**Bruce Croxon.**
**What's the Worst Thing That Can Happen.**

*Dad has a favourite expression. It was most often used when a decision had to be made or there was a chance for an opportunity to be realized. Given there is always a downside to balance the upside, Dad could be counted on to issue a final summarizing question: "What's the worst that could happen?"*

*The question was usually asked at the point where it was all but certain one was moving forward. I think it was his way of saying go for it!*

*I've heard him use this logic on himself. He came from very little and found a way to make a living and support his family's basic needs. The answer to his question was: If things go wrong I can always start again and get a job.*

*He risked it all on two occasions that I'm aware of: 1) when he got together with Mel and Deryck to start North York Chev Olds; and 2) when he parlayed that operating success into a stake in the Yonge-Steeles Auto Mall. The latter move was challenged severely by interest rates that soared above twenty percent.*

*I've relied on this creed on so many occasions and I find myself using it now with my kids. Knowing that the worst thing usually keeps you fed, healthy, and loved has taken a whole lot of pressure out of making tough decisions. I'm so grateful that Dad introduced me to this phrase.*

• • • •

And the road was bumpy in the household as well. In July 1980, Norma and Noel separated. For a while, Norma continued to live in their house and Noel moved into a furnished rented apartment.

In the business, the team was forced to reduce their expenses as much as possible. What bothered Noel most was having to lay off personnel. The dealership had to sell the four acres behind and to the west of the property in order to improve their cash position. Of all the business ventures that Noel undertook, this was the toughest one to live through. To add insult to injury, during this time Noel's income was limited, so he and Norma put their beloved Muskoka cottage up for sale.

In the early 1970s, Noel invested in an apartment rental building in Scarborough as a tax shelter to give him a write-off against his income. The building had about one-hundred and twenty rental units in it and Noel was very involved in ensuring its success: he was on its Board of Directors, and followed the financial side of the investment very closely. He discovered that the management team that ran the building, collected the rent, and sought new tenants to fill vacant apartments was not depositing the payments made by the tenants in cash. Ever frugal and practical, Noel, who was living alone at the time, obtained the approval of the board to move into the apartment building. He served as its manager and oversaw its turnaround.

. . . .

**Sheilagh Croxon.**
**Back to Basics.**

*When two people decide to end a marriage after twenty-five years, it's hard on all members of the family. This occurred in our family around 1980, just after the opening of the new dealership (North York Chev Olds at 7200 Yonge Street). My dad left the family home in search of a new dwelling. About a year after he moved out, interest rates began to soar. Cash flow was extremely tight and no one was buying cars due to the high interest rates. This meant saying goodbye to our family cottage. Dad needed the cash in order to reduce his expenses and save the business.*

*One might have thought that Dad would find it hard to give up his increasingly comfortable lifestyle. But this did not seem to faze him. He simply set about reducing his expenses to the point where he had next to none.*

*He had a business investment, a multiple unit rental business (MURB), with several other individuals. It was an apartment building located at Markham and Sheppard in Scarborough. It was intended to be a tax shelter, but the MURB was not turning a profit, primarily because the building was not being properly managed. There were numerous vacancies and a high turnover of units due to dissatisfied tenants. In an effort to reduce his personal expenses, Dad moved into the building. With the permission of the board, he fired the management and took charge of the operation.*

*This successful car dealer and respected business man was now hustling to fill vacancies, improve maintenance in the building, and search for a capable individual to run the front office. This was all done in an attempt to turn the investment into a profitable one to benefit all shareholders. He garnered interest by showcasing model suites and improving advertising. Each apartment he successfully rented brought him great satisfaction. Being a tenant himself, he had the perfect vantage point to observe on a daily basis what needed to be done to improve the resident experience. In a few short months, the building was close to one hundred percent occupancy.*

*To furnish his own unit, Dad collected second-hand furniture by answering ads in newspapers and scanning garage sales on the weekend. The basic apartment was soon furnished with the essentials at a very low cost. He lived in this apartment at Sheppard and Markham for close to five years.*

*Throughout this trial in his life, Dad showed immense humility. Money and business success had not changed him. He had quickly returned to his survival instincts and his ability to make something from nothing because that was what the situation required. There was no entitlement, no feeling sorry for himself, and absolutely no embarrassment over taking an apartment (or fulfilling the duties of a property manager) at Sheppard and Markham Square.*

*To this day, some of the antique furniture he purchased to make his own apartment a livable space still sits in my home, including the kitchen table where this book was born.*

• • • •

Noel could see that his fortunes were turning and wanted to give back. While living in the new building, he decided to volunteer with Big Brothers of Toronto. His little brother was Jason. So began a relationship that would be long-lasting.

Noel knew he had even more to offer, so while he was on the board of Big Brothers, he and three other people launched a fundraising event, called the Gourmet Dinner. At the first gala, they hosted one hundred men who paid one hundred dollars each to attend. The dinner continues on to this day, and is now called "The Big Night Out," attracting four- to five-hundred people per sitting and raising extraordinary amounts of money for Big Brothers.

In 1984, Noel was named "Big Brother of the Year," receiving much press attention and many congratulatory letters from friends. As it happened, Jason's mother was in need of a job, and she came to work for Noel at the apartment building where she executed her job with great efficiency and effectiveness.

• • • •

## Melanie Baumeister.
## Big Brother.

*Sometime in 1982 I contacted the Big Brothers hoping to find a caring man to be a positive role model for my ten-year-old son. I felt I was taking a huge risk allowing a stranger into his life. Big Brothers called me a few months later saying they had someone in mind, and Noel came into our lives.*

*The first time Noel came to pick up Jason he arrived in a red corvette convertible. It was a thrill for Jason to ride in it. Often Noel would take Jason to North York Chev Olds. Noel knew Jason's sister Kristy was terminally ill and that his father was no longer part of his life. Through the many activities they enjoyed together, Noel gave Jason experiences that helped fill voids in Jason's life.*

*For the following three years Noel provided Jason with the opportunity to go to Camp Kawabi for a month during summer break. Thanks to that excellent camp he learned many skills that have helped him in life.*

*In addition to what Noel did for Jason, he helped me as well by offering me a position at Sheppard Markham Square. It was an enjoyable experience that lasted almost ten years.*

*I will always be grateful for what Noel did for Jason, as well as for his friendship over the years.*

• • • •

Noel was pleased that, despite the breakup of his marriage, his children were engrossed and succeeding at their schooling and other endeavours: Bruce was attending Huron College in London, Ontario, and Sheilagh and Michael were at Ridley College in St. Catharines, Ontario.

With his busy children, extensive charitable involvement, property management, and thriving business, Noel's life was certainly full, but his home was quiet and still, and he longed for more.

# Chapter Thirteen

# Faith

· · · · ·

One night, Noel and his friend Mel were in a bar at the Inn on the Park following a particularly awful Maple Leafs hockey game they had left early. They were relishing the long stretches of silence in between chatter that only old friends can enjoy. Mel was reliving a particularly catastrophic penalty kill when the bartender came over and interrupted: "Excuse me, sir, but the young lady over there thinks she knows you."

Noel leaned forward and saw that at the other end of the bar a woman was peering back at him. Noel gave a brief wave and stood to walk over, tugging Mel to join him.

"Hi," she said stretching out her hand. Noel shook it, as she continued: "I'm Faith Irwin, well, I was Irwin, but I'm recently divorced, and now I go by my maiden name, Faith Paliare. I used to be married to your manager at North York, Jack Irwin."

Noel, who remembered the names and faces of everyone who had ever worked with or for him, nodded in recognition and said: "Nice to meet you, Faith."

Mel, Noel, and Faith talked until late into the night. Noel was eager to continue their discussion and asked Faith to join him for dinner a few nights later. They spoke for hours again and their friendship began to blossom. For a few years, they nurtured this new relationship, remaining friends, but sensing more was to come. Finally they took the extra step and became a couple.

Before long they purchased a cottage on Twelve Mile Lake in Minden, Ontario. It was a newly built home, not completely finished, so together they employed people to do what was needed. In the short time they owned the cottage, they enjoyed many good weekends there with relatives and friends. Occasionally Jason would join them, and learned to fish and use the rowboat.

In 1986, Noel and Faith moved in together at 85 Skymark Drive. They purchased the condominium brand-new from Tridel. That same winter, they visited Florida and bought another condo on Siesta Key. They joined a golf club there, and loved spending most of their winters down south, with Noel travelling back and forth to Toronto in order to participate on GM committees and tend to business at the dealership. He felt a growing sense of contentment.

Noel felt great satisfaction watching his now twenty-something children mature and begin to thrive at their own endeavours. Since early in his life, Bruce had exhibited strong entrepreneurial tendencies and an impressive work ethic, managing a paper route in Guildwood Village as a youngster, then paying his own way through university by taking on tough summer jobs, such as working on an oil rig. Bruce planted trees in British Columbia for several years and earned a promotion to foreman. While at Huron College, he and some friends purchased a house and rented rooms to students. When he finished university, they sold the house at a profit. Shortly after finishing his schooling, Bruce took the money he had saved and left on a trip around the world with nothing but a backpack.

After finishing high school, Sheilagh spent one year at the University of Toronto, but moved on to pursue her dream of becoming a national-level synchronized swimming coach. She spent some time in Calgary being mentored by Canada's head synchro coach, Debbie Muir. Noel supported Sheilagh's dream unconditionally, and even drove with her across the country, so that she would have a vehicle there.

In 1986, Michael was still attending university at Huron College.

• • • •

## Michael Croxon.
## The Game.

*My dad did not have the privilege of growing up playing a lot of sports and, being British, likely did not understand the Canadian obsession with hockey. As a result, we did not grow up playing Canada's game. He did, however, take a keen interest in golf once he had successfully launched his career as a car dealer. He loved the game and we played a lot together. Golf brought us closer together.*

*My first golf memories were of caddying for him at Scarborough Golf Club where he took the time to teach me the etiquette of the game and periodically allowed me to hit a ball. When I grew older, I played there and at Thornhill Country Club. My dad tolerated my temper tantrums and applauded my progress. While I cannot remember the first time I beat him, I do remember it being a very big day for me.*

*We took a trip to Virginia when I turned sixteen. The purpose was two-fold: to give me experience driving and to play golf. It was great to be away, just the two of us, deepening my affection for the game he loved to play.*

• • • •

After Bruce returned from his backpacking trip, Noel asked if he was going to join him in the business. He had a clear response: "Dad, that's your business. I want to do things for myself." He began to dabble in many different types of enterprises, some achieving mild success. One day he went to Noel with financial statements from a group that was running a dating service. Because this was prior to the advent of the Internet, the service was run via voicemail. Bruce and his business partner at the time needed to come up with ninety thousand dollars to obtain sixty percent of the business, and they had each raised thirty thousand dollars. Noel decided to invest thirty thousand for twenty percent of the business. When the Internet arrived, they took the business online, and it became a sensation. It was extremely profitable; Noel sold his shares to the other shareholders for $3.8 million. Because of this, from that point on Noel's personal life was cash flow positive, with no debts nor mortgages.

• • • •

**Bruce Croxon.**
**Of Course You Can.**

*When I was thirteen, my dad was driving me back to boarding school, which was a time that allowed for some one-on-one conversation. Cindy Nicholas had just swum Lake Ontario and we were talking about that accomplishment. What she had done inspired me and I asked my dad whether he thought it would be possible for me to swim Lake Ontario. Without hesitation he replied, "Of course you could. You can really do anything you put your mind to."*

*I believed him, perhaps because that's what boys of thirteen tend to do when their father says something. Or perhaps I trusted what he said because he had the credibility to say it. I was very familiar at that time with his story and how it was possible to start with nothing, and through hard work, sacrifice, grit and determination, achieve a lot.*

*The faith he had in me was put to the test when it came time for me to choose whether to join him in the business he had created, or pursue my dream of being an entrepreneur. I knew how badly he wanted me to join him at North York Chevrolet. We both knew that we would have been good partners.*

*He remained neutral when telling me, "If you decide to go your own way, you can make it in business," even though his desires were for me to join him in his business. It was the ultimate display of walking the talk. As I embarked on my own path, he was always there. He covered my paper route when I was sick or away. He invested scarce dollars in me when it came time to make a move on my first real company, the beginnings of Lavalife. He is still there now, inquiring how things are going and supporting me with keen interest.*

*In the past years, I have come to realize how critical confidence is in life, and I am acutely aware of where mine came from.*

• • • •

Following Sheilagh's time under the mentorship of Debbie Muir, she returned to Toronto and started a synchro club in Etobicoke, which eventually became one of the most successful in the nation, producing numerous Olympic medal winners. In 1996, Sheilagh served as assistant coach for the Canadian squad that won a silver medal at the Olympic Games in Atlanta, USA.

She then took on the Head Coach position, and led Canada to the bronze medal in the team event at the 2000 Olympic Games in Sydney, Australia. She became a sought-after consultant and coach for athletes around the world, and was elected into the Etobicoke Sports Hall of Fame in 2009.

• • • •

### Sheilagh Croxon.
### I Believe in You.

*As a young girl I was exposed to many activities, experiences and sports. In my early teens, I discovered a passion for synchronized swimming, not realizing at the time that I had uncovered a calling that would stay with me for my life time. Looking back, I wonder if this passion would ever have been realized to its full potential, had it not been for the support and encouragement of my dad.*

*I began coaching as a part time job to earn some extra money in my senior year of high school. I had come to realize that the prospect of helping other people improve their skills was more appealing and enjoyable to me than continuing to train and compete myself. I experienced what I would now characterize as immediate success working with young athletes, realizing not only that I had a gift for inspiring others but that I truly loved the challenge and the work.*

*Part way through my post-secondary studies at the University of Toronto, I announced to my dad that I had a dream: to be the best coach in the world one day, developing athletes to the highest level of the sport. I felt that I needed to leave school in order to devote my full energy and attention toward reaching this dream.*

*Many scenarios whirled around in my mind as I awaited his response. Would my announcement be taken seriously? Would I be told that I needed to honor my academic gifts and finish university? Would I be met with questions about how I could possibly make a living or gently told that the odds of reaching the highest level were slim? Any of these reactions would have been predictable from any parent. But Dad's response went something like this: "Sheilagh, I believe in you. If this is what you want to do, you have my support. How can I help you? What do you need?"*

*My heart overflowed with admiration for my father, who was already at the top of my list of incredible role models. Dad believed in me! He supported me and wanted to know how he could help! This belief strengthened my inner voice and my somewhat fragile internal belief that my dream was actually possible.*

*I believe in you. These are the four most powerful words a parent can say to a child. Thanks Dad for your belief in me, for listening to me, for helping me to listen to my inner voice and to honor my heart.*

*Thanks to you I had the courage to pursue my passion and to make my dream a reality.*

• • • •

When Michael graduated from college, he spent a year at Expo 86 in Vancouver, where he earned enough money to be able to backpack around the world for almost a year. Following his globetrotting, he joined Noel at North York in 1990, took a course with the Federation of Automobile Dealers' Association, worked in every department within the dealership, and quickly learned the business. He developed a strong relationship with both employees and customers, and was well respected by General Motors and all the associations to which he belonged. Michael assumed the responsibility of running the dealership in 1993. At this time, Noel stepped back from the business, although he kept an office at the dealership, took many vacations, and spent much of his winters with Faith in Florida.

• • • •

**Michael Croxon.**
**The Trip.**

*One of my most powerful memories of Dad involved a trip that Bruce and I took with him in 2004. We had heard the stories of his childhood so many times growing up, so we were eager to return to the London area and see the setting of that narrative. We took a few days to drive to see his childhood haunts. He showed us where his family lived while his father worked as a labourer on a farm; he brought us to the location of the airfield where he was trapped during a German bombing run in World War II; he walked us past the building where he secured his first office job; and he drove us around the countryside giving context to the multitude of stories we had heard over the years. The trip helped me appreciate more deeply how Dad has always remembered where he came from and what he had to overcome to get where he did in life.*

• • • •

Noel began to return to England annually. His mother was still living, but aging quickly. Noel generously purchased a small apartment in London and moved her into it. Both Faith and Noel would visit to spend time with her until she was moved into a Brighton nursing home in 1991.

She passed away there at the age of 93.

Noel kept himself moving. With Faith, he travelled extensively, including many cruises, several golfing excursions to Pebble Beach, Ireland, and England, and GM-related trips to Europe, Australia, New Zealand, China, Japan, and elsewhere. Faith and Noel played golf around the world. One of their favourite holidays was to British Columbia where they played all the Whistler courses, then drove to Kelowna and continued their golf adventure there. They also spent two weeks visiting all the famous courses in South Ireland. In Toronto, they honed their skills and made new friends at the Thornhill Golf Club where they were members.

The travels and seemingly endless joy stopped in May 2009 when Faith was diagnosed with non-small cell lung cancer. She underwent many trials and chemotherapy treatments at the Princess Margaret Hospital over the course of the next four-and-a-half years, losing all of her hair and suffering dreadfully through many side effects. Noel stayed close to home during this time, helping care for her. She succumbed to her illness on December 21, 2013, and continues to be missed by friends, family and, especially, Noel.

• • • •

## Chris Paliaire.
## Loving Faith.

*Over thirty years ago, Noel came into my life when he married my sister, Faith. He quickly became an integral part of our family. During all the years I've known Noel, he has been a loving and doting uncle to our daughters Zoë and Julia, both of whom adore their "Uncle Noelie."*

*When most people think of Noel, they think of him as an amazing humanitarian, and superb businessman who built an enormously successful business, despite all its attendant risks. He is a kind and thoughtful leader; a person who recognizes the importance of philanthropy, giving back to the community and helping those less fortunate.*

*The Noel I want to talk about is the person who responded to adversity with incredible and unwavering commitment. The true measure of a person is not how well they react when things are going well, but rather what stuff they're made of when things do not go as planned I recall the day that Noel, Faith and I were summoned to Princess Margaret Hospital to be told that Faith had stage four small cell lung cancer, and that there was no known cure for it. The news was devastating. Noel and Faith had enjoyed their lives together, golfing, spending winters in Florida and travelling the world. The health news put the lives they had known and enjoyed on hold, as it turned out, forever. Now their energies would be devoted to assisting Faith through this difficult, perilous and unknown journey.*

*From that point until Faith passed away on December 21, 2013, Noel did everything possible to comfort and encourage Faith through her many chemotherapy treatments and experimental trials. Noel made the meals, did the grocery shopping and chauffeured to and from doctor appointments and hospitals. He assumed these duties quickly and without complaint.*

*Noel's efforts to assist Faith went well beyond what would have been expected of anyone. He did so not for any recognition or sense of obligation. Rather, he knew it was what needed to be done and he demonstrated extreme patience and devotion during the most trying of circumstances.*

*His role over the last three years of Faith's life is ingrained in my memory and reinforces the simple fact that Noel is truly an outstanding human being who has made a difference in the lives of so many.*

• • • •

# Chapter Fourteen

# Crossing the Ocean

· · · · ·

In June 2014, Noel, Sheilagh, and Noel's granddaughters, Natalie and Marley, decided to take a trip together to London to visit the geography of Noel's childhood. While Sheilagh booked flights, Noel purchased a passage by ship. It would be one of those full circle moments: he would travel back to the land of his birth, with all his memories and experiences stowed in the deepest parts of him. On the day of his departure, Sheilagh handed him ninety-two dollars, once all he had, now mere pocket change, which he tucked away in his coat pocket, feeling its reassuring weight and significance. He had reserved a first-class stateroom, a rewarding step up from the cabin below deck he had shared during his emigration over fifty years earlier.

Noel boarded the ship that June day, stepping off the soil

of the nation where he had now spent more than half his life, and spared no time before looking out to sea. Across there, somewhere, was the place where he had been born into relative poverty, to parents who had loved him but struggled to love one another, who strove to provide stability, but ended up introducing Noel to constant movement. It was during those earlier years that Noel discovered the power of taking life into his own hands and working hard; where he unlocked the potential of his mind; tasted the first thrills and dangers of adventure; found companionship and felt it slip through his fingers; found it again and chased it (and hope) to a new land. Now he was heading back there, armed with confidence. The urge to keep moving onward still pulsed within him, but it was less frantic now.

He stared out at the line of whitecaps in the distance. No crossing is ever smooth, but he knew the secret of any passage now: head directly into those waves, those bumps in the road, those hills and obstacles, gain traction, and keep on going.

Words without action are like wheels without traction.
It is how you live that counts.

Geoff Thompson

# Full Speed Ahead

· · · · ·

## Sheilagh's Kitchen. September 25, 2015

*"I have never needed a gold ring. It's important to some people, but not me. We are all different. I grew up with nothing, never needed material things to make me feel good about myself, and I don't need them now. Having good relationships with people, giving, feeling good about yourself, that's what's important in life, not material things."* These were the simple but powerful words of advice Noel imparted to his granddaughter Marley as we sat around the kitchen table for dinner one September evening.

Noel can still be found in the back office of the dealership a few mornings each week, going over his to-do list. He's still eager to make a positive contribution whether through a story, a customer handshake, or providing a hot cup of coffee. He is always interested in hearing about the weekly sales of new and used cars, and the general manager looks forward to Noel's weekly call at the end of every Saturday. As Noel approaches his 90th birthday, we celebrate the traction he has made in influencing the lives of others, most notably his three children.

When Michael officially transitioned to the role of Dealer Principal of North York Chevrolet Oldsmobile in 1997, Noel immediately gave up his corner office, allowing his son and successor to take over the helm. Today, Michael is the founder and President of NewRoads Automotive, which over the past two decades has acquired and sold numerous dealerships. He currently owns five stores in the Greater Toronto Area (GM, Chrysler, Suburu, and Mazda). He is among the most respected leaders in the automotive industry, and acknowledges the role Noel has played in offering invaluable guidance and support at every stage of his career. In a recent media interview, he described Noel "as a great leader of people, who does so in an understated way, devoid of ego."

• • • •

## A Letter from a Dealership Employee.
## October 2010.

*Dear Noel,*

*Words cannot express how thankful I am to have had this opportunity to work for someone with as much class and style as you. It is something few people will ever experience. This is the reason why most of your employees are willing to go out of their way for you, and for Michael and his new venture.*

*I remember the days when you would wander through the shop, stop and talk to each of us. I would think, "Wow! The president of this company cares about me!"*

*From time to time I've seen you plunge the bathroom sink or pick up garbage as you walk by. You have shown by example that no matter your position in life, no job is beneath you. I have told the story, how you once told me before I left for holidays, that if something was to go wrong, I should call you and you would get me home. Then you handed me twenty pounds for my stopover in London. The response to the story was: "That's just Noel, and he means it, too!"*

*To us in the shop you have become the definition of what a good person is. I am overwhelmed by your compassion and concern for the people that have worked for you. You have shown a level of professionalism that we strive for.*

*Thank You.*

• • • •

Since the sale of Lavalife in 2004 and leaving the company in 2006, Bruce currently helms Round 13 Capital, a company dedicated to investing in growth stage digital companies. Noel did not miss an episode of CBC's Dragons Den during the three seasons Bruce appeared on the show, and faithfully watches the weekly episode of *The Disruptors* on BNN where Bruce is the co-host. On more than one occasion in the past year, Bruce has invited Noel on stage during his keynotes to various organizations, both to acknowledge Noel as a key influencer in his life and to have him share his wisdom with the audience.

After stepping down as head coach of Canada's National Synchronized Swimming team in 2002, Sheilagh turned her attention to advancing the profession of coaching while continuing to develop her knowledge as an athlete development expert. As a leading advocate for women in coaching, she has designed and championed numerous initiatives aimed at increasing and retaining women in the profession. She continues to consult as a subject matter expert with sport organizations worldwide and at all levels of the Canadian Sport System.

It is often a challenge to impart values and life lessons to the third generation. Through sharing Noel's life story, we hope to have conveyed some key lessons, including the importance of hard work, determination, risk-taking, supporting others, and trusting your inner voice. And, above all, to keep moving.

And the last word goes to Noel...

••••

**Noel Croxon.**
**Letter to Grandchildren.**

*October 13, 2014*

*To Sarah, Grace, Anna, Addy, Lucas, Marley, Natalie, and Nicolas,*

*First, I want to let you know that I love you all very, very much. Second, I hope that you all live and enjoy your lives to the fullest. I hope you all reach and achieve the things you plan for and dream of. As you all know, I personally had very little in material things and lived in poor conditions while growing up in England. I left school at the age of 14 years, in 1941.*

*What I want you all to know is that material things don't really make you happy. It's all about love, caring, and giving that will make you happy in your lives. You are all growing up and the years go by very quickly, and before you know it, you will all be older.*

*Now, the really important stuff ... you will all become parents one day and you will have that baby and hold it in your arms for the first time. Wow! Your life and your worries and concerns will change on that day. Your major focus will be on that baby plus any others you have later.*

*The parent-child relationship is hard to understand until you yourself experience it. So please try and understand that any rules and restrictions your parents place on you is because they love you, and will do so and protect you for the rest of their lives ... just as you will do when you have your families.*

*You may now say that I'm wrong, but when the day comes and you are a parent, and you hold that baby in your arms, you will say: "Grampa was right."*

*Love,*
*Grampa*
*xoxox*

• • • •

Bruce, Noel, Norma, Sheilagh, Pam and Ken Miller
1963

Bruce, Noel, Michael, Norma and Sheilagh
1973

Cran Jr., Yvonne, Leo and Noel
1981

Noel and Jo
Visiting England, circa 1980

Noel and Cran Jr.
Outside the
Epping Green House
1980's

Faith outside the Lawrence Cottage
Great Waldingfield, England
1987

OFFICE OF
VICE-PRESIDENT AND DIRECTOR OF SALES

January 17, 1969

Mr. Noel Croxon,
North York Chevrolet Oldsmobile Ltd.,
5642 Yonge Street,
Willowdale, Ontario.

Dear Noel:

May I take this opportunity to officially welcome you
into the General Motors Dealer Organization.

From your previous experience you understand well enough
our pride in their progressiveness, accomplishments and
splendid reputation.

And, we are grateful that there exists between us such a
high standard of confidence, co-operation and good under-
standing.

It will be our purpose to help you in every way possible
and you may, consequently, rely upon our Management and
Representatives, whenever any assistance is desired.

Please accept my sincerest wishes for a pleasant and alto-
gether successful relationship.

Very sincerely yours,

L. A. Hastings
blc

Letter from L.A. Hastings
Vice President and Director of Sales, General Motors Canada
1969

Beginnings of North York Chevrolet

Toronto Auto Centre
1975

# HE TURNED $93.00 INTO MILLIONS

*"I will not accept mediocrity"*

North York Business News
May 1989

## With a handful of change and a pocketful of large dreams

by Robert Leonard

In 1956 a young man arrived in Canada with only $92 in cash, but a pocketful of dreams.

This year, at 61, Noel Croxon celebrates his 20th year as president of North York Chev-Olds after 33 years of hard work and dedication to his community.

He has served as president of the Rotary Club; Toronto Auto Dealers Association; Toronto Auto Show; General Motors Dealer Association and received recognition as Time Magazine Quality Dealer and Big Brother of the Year in 1988.

Croxon began his climb up the corporate ladder by taking a job as office manager at Robertson Motors on Danforth Ave. for $70 per week. Scrimping and saving, he worked at Alex Irvine

continued on page 9

## With $92 in cash

continued from page 1 Motors from 1963 to 1968, then, with a group of investors, purchased North York Chev-Olds at Yonge and Finch in Willowdale.

Six years later the dealership moved to the old Loblaws' location on 18 acres of land at Yonge and Steeles, and Croxon formulated a plan to turn the area into a comprehensive automotive business centre.

From his office window, a part of the old grocery store is still visible, though unrecognizable — it's now incorporated into a modern auto showroom.

By 1980 Croxon bought out his co-investors and became partners with Roy Foss. Together they developed the auto park now known as the Toronto Automobile Centre.

North York Chev-Olds opened in 1981 and moved out of the original building to a new complex designed under Croxon's direction. And the Toronto Automobile Centre is now home to North York Chevrolet Oldsmobile, Roy Foss Pontiac Buick Cadillac, Town & Countrye Motors and Willowdale Nissan.

Claiming he is semi-retired, and fit, trim and relaxed at 61, Croxon is still planning for the future of his business.

Croxon credits his success to a great deal of hard work, and good working relationships with both employees and customers to develop trust and loyalty.

What he may not recognize as possibly the major factor, is his self-confessed inability to tolerate mediocrity.

The Canadian International Auto Show
recognizes the valued contributions and
efforts of its illustrious Past Presidents:

| | | | |
|---|---|---|---|
| 1974 | W.J. Shanahan | 1987 | Ed Nimeck |
| 1975 | Ross Wemp | 1988 | Don Strupat |
| 1976 | Wes Scott | 1989 | Craig Hind |
| 1977 | Noel Croxon | 1990 | Harry Lawson |
| 1978 | Bill Popovich | 1991 | Bill McArthur |
| 1979 | Claude Frost | 1992 | Bill Nurse |
| 1980 | John Bear | 1993 | Bob Attrell |
| 1981 | Bob Foster | 1994 | John Carmichael |
| 1982 | Len Sanci | 1995 | Bob Stephen |
| 1983 | Bryan Rowntree | 1996 | John Longman |
| 1984 | Peter Menzel | 1997 | John Longman |
| 1985 | Dalt Ouderkirk | 1998 | Gordon Wilson |
| 1986 | Nick Bozian | | |

We take the opportunity on this our 25th Anniversary
to honour them for all their endeavours.

Canadian International Auto Show
List of Presidents
1998

Scarborough Mirror / R.D. FULLER

SCARBOROUGH RESIDENT and Big Brother Noel Croxon, right, shares the limelight with his little brother, Jason. Croxon was named the 1988 Big Brother of the Year for Metro at a special ceremony at the Royal York Hotel Sunday. He'll represent the agency throughout 1988, its 75th anniversary.

# Metro's biggest brother hails from Scarborough

**By ANTONELLA ARTUSO**
**Staff Reporter**

A Scarborough man has been named the 1988 Big Brother of the Year, Metro's most important tribute to a volunteer.

Noel Croxon, also named Scarborough's Big Brother of the Year, earned his accolade through 18 years of dedicated service to the organization. Croxon, who turns 60 on Christmas Day, has spent the last four years as big brother to 15-year-old Jason.

"Right from the start," said Jason's mother, "Noel has been concerned with every aspect of Jason's life, from his school work and his co-operation at home to his sporting activities. During our very difficult time some months ago, when my daughter died, Jason knew Noel was there for him and that meant a lot for both of us."

Now Jason says he intends to be a Big Brother "because I have gotten such a great feeling about everything that I would like to share it with other young kids."

Eighteen years ago, Croxon helped found the agency's fund-raising Gourmet Dinner and single-handedly helped raise more than $250,000 for the program.

As the 1988 Metro Award winner, Croxon received the Inglis Trophy and an Inglis appliance of his choice. He also received a plaque from the Allstate Insurance Company as did all area winners.

Croxon will represent Big Brothers throughout the next 12 months, the agency's 75 anniversary year. For information on how to become a Big Brother, call 925-8981.

Scarborough Mirror
1988

Big Brother Dinner
Michael, Bruce, Noel and Sheilagh
November 2015

Noel and Jason

## A celebration for Noel's 90th birthday held on December 21, 2017

. . . . .

With Michael, Sheilagh, Bruce

With his grandchildren
Marley, Anna, Sarah, Natalie, Addy, Noel, Nicolas, Lucas, Grace

With Chris Paliaire

## Bruce's toast for
## Noel's 90th birthday celebration

. . . . .

There was once a boy from North Weald,
Who was good at numbers and yield.
He grew up with nothin'
Ate rabbits and mutton,
And in here his story's revealed.

Twelve: the age of Noel's first gig,
Delivering milk on his bicycle rig.
School he found easy, but war got in the way.
So he finished grade eight, then called it a day.

While still a young man he met a maiden Jamaican.
Low and behold he became good and taken.
Off to Canada in a boat barely lit,
Hoping that Norma would organize some shit!

Located in Toronto to start life anew,
Out popped yours truly, Sheilagh and then Uncle Stu.
Oh, how the latter two did fight,
Leaving Bruce, the first born, and still favour"I"te.

The opportunities were many,
The business climate was swell.
Noel built a great business
With Gilpie and Mel.
His passion was golf,
He played pretty great.
The drives never went far,
But boy they were straight!

His other passion was Faith,
A love taken too soon,
Memories to cherish
From here to the moon.

You grandkids take note:
With a story like this,
Make the most of your talent,
No matter what it is.

It's not the dog in the fight,
But the fight in the dog.
Work hard at your craft
Because life is a slog.

And so here we are, 90 years on.
Three 30's, nine 10's, ten 9's and so on.
Whatever way you slice it, this stage starts with a nine,
So enough said by me, let's all drink some wine!

Fill your life with experiences, not things.

Have stories to tell, not stuff to show.

Author Unknown

## Noel Croxon
## Noteworthy Achievements

. . . . .

Awarded a General Motors Franchise. 1968

North Scarborough Rotary Club, President. 1974

Toronto Dealers Association, President. 1976

International Car Show, President. 1977

Toronto General Motors Dealers Association, President. 1982

Big Brother of the Year for Metropolitan Toronto. 1985

Recognized by General Motors of Canada
for 50 years as a General Motors Dealer. 2018

## Personal stories shared by:

**Michael Croxon**
Noel's son

**Bruce Croxon**
Noel's son

**Sheilagh Croxon**
Noel's daughter

**Deryck Gilpin**
Noel's brother in law (Norma's brother)

**Chris Paliaire**
Noel's brother in law (Faith's brother)

**Mel Smirle**
Noel's business partner and friend

**Melanie Baumeister**
Mother of Jason (Noel's little brother)

Bobby Orr, Jan Wilson, Faith and Noel
Pebble Beach, 1990's